More Praise for *High-Payoff Strategies*

"Jody Spiro has taken a complex subject and made it highly useful.... If a school leader wants to make a difference, she will adhere to the strategies defined in this book. From visioning to implementation, this book will lead the way, and our students will be the ultimate winners."

—*Diane Rutledge, Executive Director, Large Unit District Association (LUDA), Springfield, Illinois*

"Mahalo for High-Payoff Strategies. The book has helped me develop our faculty and create a sharing culture that fosters better learning for students."

—*Kim Sanders, Principal, Aiea High School, Oahu, Hawaii*

High-Payoff Strategies

High-Payoff Strategies

How Education Leaders Get Results

Jody Spiro

Published by Jossey-Bass
A Wiley Brand
One Montgomery Street, Suite 1000, San Francisco, CA 94104–4594—www.josseybass.com

Library of Congress Cataloging-in-Publication Data
Spiro, Jody, author.
  High-payoff strategies : how education leaders get results / Jody Spiro.
    pages cm
  Includes bibliographical references and index.
  ISBN 978-1-118-83441-1 (pbk.), 978-1-118-84193-8 (ePDF), 978-1-118-84191-4 (ePUB)
  1. Educational leadership. 2. Educational innovations. 3. Educational change. I. Title.
  LB2806.S6517 2015
  371.2--dc23

                                            2015030928

Cover design by Wiley
Cover photograph © Ron Chapple Stock|Thinkstock

Printed in the United States of America
FIRST EDITION
PB Printing   10 9 8 7 6 5 4 3 2 1

Contents

PART 4   The Payoff 117

Acknowledgments

When I set out on the journey many years ago that led to this book, I had reams of data from interviewing education leaders and hearing their feedback on the tools I had developed. But I was at a loss for the best way to help others use this information. Whereas my first book was designed for change leaders in a variety of nonprofit sectors, after it was published I got feedback that a second book was needed—aimed specifically at leaders in education. As many education leaders attempted to use the techniques in the first book, they asked me questions more specifically related to their practice. I then understood the value of the book you are about to read. Whereas *Leading Change Step-by-Step* outlined general tools and techniques and provided examples from several sectors, *High-Payoff Strategies: How Education Leaders Get Results* takes those general tools and lessons and makes them specific for immediate application by education leaders.

I did not come to this realization on my own. I had continual feedback from many dedicated education leaders who were using the materials and found them valuable yet did not hesitate to let me know how they could be improved and what additional material was needed. Therefore, many thanks to those critical friends: Andy Cole, Mark Shellinger, and those participating in the National SAM Innovation Project; Glenn Pethel and the group of principals from Gwinnett County; Douglas Anthony and the principals of Prince George's County; Tricia McManus and the principals from Hillsborough County; Ann Clark and Jevelyn Bonner-Reid from Charlotte-Mecklenburg; Tom Boasberg and Mikel Royal from Denver—and all my colleagues in New York City, including Marina Cofield and chancellor Carmen Fariña.

Although the ideas in this book are my own, I have benefitted from the support and insights of my colleagues at Wallace. I owe special thanks to our president, Will Miller, who always tries to eliminate obstacles to getting good work done. He, Lucas Held, Jessica Schwartz, and Edward Pauly have been important thought partners throughout.

I received much needed encouragement from many people. I'd especially like to thank Linda Cantillano, Simon Fenster, Gay Green Steinhorn, Cindy Green, Anne DiGiovanni, Nicholas Pelzer, Rochelle Herring, Aiesha Eleusizov, Carolina Velasquez, Christine Kudrav, and Abby Spiro.

Of course, to my editor at Jossey-Bass, Margie McAneny: thanks for nudging me most diplomatically to get this done and for always making my work better.

About the Author

Jody Spiro, EdD, is director of education leadership at The Wallace Foundation. There she leads an interdisciplinary team that sponsors work across the country to learn lessons about how effective education leadership might lead to improved results for school districts, states, and students.

Her career has spanned work in education and change leadership with schools, districts, nonprofits, and governments in the United States and abroad. Prior to joining Wallace, Spiro held leadership positions at large organizations in the private, public, nonprofit, university, philanthropic, and international sectors. These included the Chancellor's Office at New York City Department of Education and senior level positions at the Soros Foundations, Long Island University, and Education Development Center, Inc. She has seen firsthand that the approaches in this book apply in all these venues. In all these positions she always has tried to walk the talk of the ideas presented in this book.

Spiro presents frequently on the topics of change leadership and education leadership at conferences held by organizations such as the American Association of School Administrators, The Council of Chief State School Officers, Learning Forward, and The Wallace Foundation. She is the author of *Leading Change Step-by-Step: Tactics, Tools, and Tales* (Jossey-Bass, 2011).

Dedicated to Lana Spiro, Estelle Green,
and Abby Gross—with gratitude to my role models

High-Payoff Strategies

Chapter 1

Introduction to the High-Payoff Strategies

Effective education leaders are important and impactful. They are responsible for leading teaching and learning throughout a school or an entire school district. They are central to how well teachers facilitate instruction and how much students learn. Education leaders therefore influence the quality of students' present and future lives and indeed the quality of the future citizenry of the community, state, and nation.

This book is the result of input from hundreds of education leaders (urban, suburban, and rural) during the past twenty years. They have described how they have successfully led important changes in their schools, organizations, and districts — and what challenges remain about which they would like advice and models. They are also asking for resources from others who have had success in bringing about changes that have made their districts and schools more effective as learning organizations not only for the students but also for the adults who work there as well. This book offers just that.

Often referred to as "second only to teaching" among school-related factors influencing student learning, leaders influence the conditions under which all instruction takes place and, therefore, have an even greater impact than that. For, although most school variables, considered separately, have small effects on learning, effective leadership can pull the pieces together into a whole that is greater than the sum of its parts. And several surveys of teachers have found that the number one factor that affects their satisfaction — or lack thereof — is school leadership.

When teachers are more satisfied, they teach better and student learning increases. Researchers at the Universities of Minnesota and Toronto demonstrated empirically the link between school leadership and improved student achievement. In fact, the research found that "to date … we have not found a single case of a school improving its student achievement record in the absence of talented leadership" (Louis et al., 2010, p. 9). The role of school leaders at all levels is important indeed.

FOCUS ON HIGH-PAYOFF STRATEGIES

An education leader's job can be overwhelming, but it doesn't have to be! What we learn from research and successful leaders is that spending time on high-payoff strategies is the best way to get the biggest bang for the buck. There are so many things to get done; it is of utmost importance to make distinctions between what needs to be done personally by the leader and what can be done by others.

Educators are often bad at making these distinctions among their plentiful tasks—they're all important to the functioning of the school or district, right? Indeed, they are, but the leader does not have to—and should not—do them all personally. An education leader is not a soloist but rather the conductor of an orchestra in which talented professionals contribute varied instruments and skills. In order to achieve this aim, two things have to happen. The leader has to identify high-payoff strategies and then devote time and attention to them—delegating other activities.

What are high-payoff strategies? Those that get the biggest results from the effort expended and pave the way to other important changes. For example, this means that education leaders need to support primarily the learning needs of the *adults* who work in schools—as opposed to the students. Although most education leaders have had gratifying and successful experiences as educators of students, the role of leaders is to mobilize the talents of the adults, who in turn work with the students. Effective leaders influence others, motivating them to contribute to the goals of the school and district.

The Starting Points

Perhaps the most important aspect of being an effective leader are having a clear vision and being relentless in its pursuit. It is essential to clearly articulate the endgame and be consistent in aligning everything that happens to getting this done. It is, further, crucial to keep at it despite the obstacles that will undoubtedly come up. Persistence is essential.

This includes ongoing monitoring of progress and midcourse corrections that will become necessary as events progress.

As the saying goes, "If you don't know where you're going, any road will take you there." Starting with a vision is imperative to leading the school or district toward success. Having a vision is meant to inspire and mobilize everyone toward the aim of high expectations for all members of the school community, especially high achievement for the students. Formulating a vision involves widespread consultation, communication, and commitment across the community.

Once the vision is clear to the leader and to the community, the effective leader personally engages, encourages the active engagement and leadership of others, aligns resources to the vision, and monitors its accomplishment through the use of data and milestones. Once the vision and focus are clear, there are three well-known, high-payoff strategies identified by research and successful principals to use in leading change in schools and districts:

- Creating a culture supportive of teaching and learning
- Leading instructional improvements
- Facilitating learning communities

Creating a Culture Supportive of Teaching and Learning

Culture represents the shared values of everyone in the school or district and how those are expressed in everything that is done on a daily basis. This is sometimes also called *climate*. It enables all staff to be part of a community striving for similar group goals—focused on student learning—through the work they each do individually and on various teams.

A culture develops organically, but it also can be led. People's real values find expression as well as those instruction-centered values deliberately infused by the leader. Research shows that principals of schools with high teacher ratings for "instructional climate are also principals who rank highest when it comes to developing an atmosphere of caring and trust" (Louis et al., 2010, p. 77).

In addition, researchers at Vanderbilt University have found that "the research over the last quarter century has consistently supported the notion that having high expectations for all, including clear and public standards, is one key to closing the achievement gap between advantaged and less advantaged students, and for raising the overall academic standards of all students" (Porter et al., 2008, p. 13).

Some aspects of culture are clearly visible (such as bulletin boards, shared language and history, and assemblies and other ceremonies and rituals). Other characteristics are evident when one knows what to look for (such as norms of staff and student behavior). Still, many cultural traits are hidden and based on assumptions that aren't spoken but are acted on. These include the real values (as opposed to those that are espoused or given lip service) and beliefs (such as whether all children are capable of high achievement). Beliefs have the most influence on the functioning of the school or district — yet they are the most difficult to identify and even more difficult, although not impossible, to change. There are many ways that great school leaders inculcate a vision into daily life of the school: celebrating teacher and student success, modeling the values that are important, and bringing student and staff opinions into decision making.

Leading Instructional Improvements

At the heart of the mission of all schools and districts is excellent instruction on the part of the educators and insightful and useful learning on the part of the students. Clearly, improving teaching and learning consistently throughout the school and district is a high-payoff strategy for any education leader. Because this mission has to be achieved through mobilizing the talents of tens — if not hundreds — of educators who collectively teach thousands, this is challenging work indeed because it encompasses skills development and implementation on both group and individual levels.

Educational success requires leadership skills including knowledge of current standards and content and development of leaders who have these attributes; knowledge of how to effectively conduct instruction (pedagogy); and the ability to lead the planning, implementation, and evaluation of large-scale strategies to identify and address the strengths and development opportunities of all staff on individual and group levels. It is important that the development of such activities widely and actively engage educators in collaborative planning.

Great leaders are thought partners with teachers in improving curriculum and instructional practices. They visit classrooms, not to monitor but as a source for coaching and mentoring ideas. They provide substantive feedback to teachers and participate in grade-level or subject-specific planning meetings.

Facilitating Learning Communities

Another high-payoff strategy for leaders that directly correlates with improving student achievement is developing and conducting ongoing learning communities for the school and district educators. In many ways, this strategy is the culmination of having created the culture and activities for improving teaching and learning. This strategy is ongoing and results oriented: the community defines and contributes model practices, tools, curriculum, or other agreed-on products for use by the community and for others in the school or district.

Research demonstrates that when leaders foster such learning communities, instruction and student achievement improves. "Leadership effects on student achievement occur largely because leadership strengthens professional community—a special environment in which teachers work together to improve their practice and improve student learning .... Professional community, in turn, is a strong predictor of instructional practices that are strongly associated with student achievement" (Louis et. al., 2010, p. 37).

The characteristics of such a community are that it be an integral part of the school and district's overall mission, whereby lessons are jointly developed between the leaders and other educators. There must be an ongoing series of coordinated learning activities for a defined set of committed members with a specific purpose and outcomes that meet a predetermined strategic objective. Therefore, essential practices include ensuring a climate of trust and respect, making sure there is immediate application of learning to solve common problems, contributing knowledge and evidence to the common work, and creating learning that is responsive to developing needs.

BUILDING BLOCKS THAT MAKE HIGH-PAYOFF STRATEGIES WORK

Once leaders have selected a high-payoff strategy to pursue, research and practitioners have identified three building blocks needed to get the desired results:

- Get buy-in: "We're all in this together."

  Principals report that staff often thinks everything is the principal's problem to solve. It is really the opposite. Effective leaders communicate that there are roles for everyone. It's everyone's job to help students learn, although each person may play a different role. Research supports this contention. "Compared with lower-achieving schools, higher-achieving schools provided all stakeholders with greater influence on decisions. Principals willing to share leadership benefit from the collective knowledge and wisdom in their school communities" (Louis et al, 2010, p. 35).

- Start with an early win.

  Momentum can be gained by starting off with an early demonstration of concrete results to persuade doubters that there is benefit in the chosen approach. Leaders will want to identity an activity that is valued by those involved that can be accomplished within the first month of the new work. The early win should be tangible and observable: non-threatening to those who may oppose the larger strategy and perceived by most people to have more benefits than costs.

The results should be symbolic of something highly valued by most group members and publicized so all become convinced that this work is achievable and will lead to the accomplishment of the larger strategy.

- Provide ongoing support.

A common mistake leaders make is to initiate important changes and assume that those who are involved in the new work have the skills to carry them out. That might (or might not) be true at the beginning—but it is assuredly not the case moving forward. Skills development is not a one-time occurrence. Once something is learned, it doesn't mean that someone has that skill forever. Change is continual; we must all continually refresh our skills and perspectives— staying ahead of the curve.

Everyone, no matter how experienced, needs continual support in the forms of coaching, feedback, and professional development. Professional athletes know this, which is why they have a full complement of coaches and ongoing training.

A WORD ABOUT EFFECTIVE CHANGE LEADERSHIP

Ultimately, this book is about leading change effectively to improve education for students and the adults who provide their instruction. It relies on techniques that have been discussed in a variety of sources, including this author's 2011 book, *Leading Change Step-by-Step: Tactics, Tools, and Tales*.

The high-payoff strategies are—at their heart—change strategies. This is crucial to consider because change has distinctive characteristics that require specific leadership techniques. *Change* in this case means something different from what is—change is a moving target, constant and continuous. It is a series of destinations that lead to further destinations. Therefore, defining milestones along the way is important or the leader will be working endlessly toward an out-of-reach goal.

In addition, change makes most people anxious. They wonder if they will have the needed skills—and also tend to hear the need to change as blaming. "If I was doing a good job, why am I being asked to change?" Because change is something different, the outcome cannot be predicted with 100 percent certainty. Therefore, it is of importance to prove the value of the new effort as soon as possible. This is often accomplished by purposefully building in an early win as described in this chapter.

Finally, because the outcome can't be predicted with certainty, leading change requires constant monitoring and revision. This requires a mind-set that it is not a mistake if course corrections have to be made—that is to be expected of a good change process. As district and school leaders use these techniques over several years, the importance of the various steps becomes apparent.

Beginning any effort to disrupt the status quo (the type of change we are after) must begin with assessing the readiness of all those involved to pursue this endeavor. Is everyone able to demonstrate the enthusiasm and skills to try—and keep at it? Will they be able to put any previous, bad experiences aside? Of course this applies as much to the leader as to the participants.

If people's readiness is low, it doesn't mean scrapping the initiative; it just means that the leader needs to provide lots of structure in what is proposed: for example, agendas, templates, and guidelines. Once participants experience success by using the structured activities, they will be ready for more autonomy. It is unfortunate that many leaders do not take this first step. Omit it at your peril! Those who do not assess and accommodate readiness often have to return to square one after much unproductive wheel-spinning.

It is then essential to assess the motivations of the various groups and individuals whose support will be needed—or who have the power to thwart the effort. Strategies should be designed to engage those whose support is necessary. Try to minimize resistance but be prepared to tolerate some. Engage people in collaborative planning and always keep an eye on the sustainability of what is being accomplished. Even if the work is successful, it won't mean much if it doesn't last. And, remember that change is continual. It is therefore essential to periodically reassess how things are going with an eye to tweaking or even changing course.

Leading any effective change process requires the ongoing analysis of accurate and timely data. What you measure matters! And, it is important to use multiple measures every time. Most of us have opinions—but do we have the *evidence* to support them or are we making assumptions based exclusively on our own ways of looking at the world? In order to ensure that we have a realistic picture of all aspects of whatever issue is being addressed, it is necessary to have data from a variety of sources to inform the discussion and decisions.

Often, however, the hardest thing to do when leading change is to identify the high-payoff strategy to pursue. Leaders need to identify where they want to go and what strategy will best take them there. In this book, that important first step is accomplished.

ORGANIZATION OF THIS BOOK

This book details three high-payoff strategies by which effective education leaders get results and how the building blocks described in this chapter come into play—building effective change leadership in each. The descriptions include examples of how successful leaders have put the strategy into action, and each strategy references a video that follows two principals who are using the strategy. The high-payoff strategy chapters also describe what can get in the way of success. Forewarned is forearmed!

Chapter 2 sets the foundation for all the strategies—how to set the vision and develop an unrelenting focus. There are descriptions, videos, and a tool.

Chapters 3 through 8 are paired chapters; each pair describes one of the high-payoff strategies. The first chapter of the pair describes the strategy, gives examples of how effective leaders have used it, references a video of it in action, and provides guidance on what can go wrong. The second chapter for each high-payoff strategy provides a tool by which data can be gathered and methods of data analysis that can contribute to planning strategy.

Chapter 9 provides specific examples of how successful education leaders have combined all three high-payoff strategies to achieve their visions.

Also included are suggestions for using the book's content in courses and workshops for education leaders as well as an annotated bibliography of sources.

Chapter 2

Vision and Focus

The Starting Points

> Lots of initiatives are not always a good thing. You need to select the ones that are really helping.
>
> —A middle school principal

One principal recently commented that bumps and bruises are part of any meaningful change process. Indeed, this is to be expected. There are many obstacles along the way (some predictable and others that will surprise), but one well-known aspect of change is that people cannot cope with too many changes at one time. Simultaneous reforms can be overwhelming even for people who like change. Fortunately, effective leaders can compensate for this.

It is of the utmost importance for an education leader to be selective about the number of changes pursued at any given time. Once a limited number of changes have been identified (preferably only one at a time) all focus must be given to their individual pursuit. More typically there are multiple reforms and many mixed messages to be given priority. They cannot all be done with always-limited resources. Picking the one or two that, once accomplished, will facilitate the others is crucial.

Here's an example: one otherwise excellent district leader always confused his colleagues each September with a back-to-school address designed to inspire them with the goals for the upcoming year. Few could argue that everything articulated was important, but—by the time he got to the *seventh* and *eighth* priorities, the audience was lost. What were they supposed to do? Were they to focus on dropout prevention? Improved test scores in reading and math? Improved student attendance? Parental engagement? Improved physical education? Better nutrition in student lunches? Opening health clinics in the middle and high schools? Adding foreign language for all secondary students? Getting all students to read twenty-five books each semester? All worthy efforts, no doubt. However, it would be impossible to concentrate on all without diluting time, attention, and resources. And, of course, none would actually be accomplished.

But, not only do successful education leaders identify a limited number of priorities and demonstrate total commitment to their accomplishment but also focus on money, people, and time to achieve their successful implementation. It also means not giving up, persisting despite the obstacles that arise, revising the plan to meet new circumstances, and giving it full attention. By doing this, not only will the first priority be accomplished but also momentum will be built for the accomplishment of future reforms.

That's why, before going on to subsequent chapters, it is necessary to discuss vision and focus. These are indispensable factors for the success of all initiatives.

SETTING THE VISION

Perhaps the best description of the importance of setting a vision comes from a group of eight principals from five districts who recently wrote a handbook for other principals after reflecting on what they thought their colleagues would most want when developing such a roadmap (GLISI, 2013).

The group found these indispensable elements:

- Developing the vision by getting input from staff members
- Collaborating with the school leadership team
- Imagining the inspirational future state of the school or district
- Recognizing the common direction of growth

The vision should be "inspirational and aspirational" and should communicate what the school hopes to achieve (GLISI, 2013, p. 7). Of course, communicating the vision is important, but it must be translated into action. As an elementary school principal observes, "The vision needs to be more than a catchphrase. The vision has to be lived day in and day out."

Why is the vision so important? Here's a success story told by an elementary principal:

> A few years ago, I received a card from one of our school's best teachers. The note was a "thank you" for challenging her to continuously improve her performance. For years, this teacher outperformed her colleagues, consistently receiving exemplary evaluations and achievement results. I was surprised to read that the teacher was considering transferring to another school before I arrived but that the development of the school vision, and, more important, observing me holding myself and others accountable to the vision, encouraged her to stay. Once she was convinced that the school leadership team was serious about our vision, she challenged herself to be serious about it too. She went on to become not only a leader in our school but also a leader in our district. (p. 6)

The vision as expressed by another elementary school principal is "I see my job as preparing children for opportunities that haven't even been created yet." Of course, the goal is not only to have a well-developed and aspirational vision statement for the school but also to have it align with the aspirational vision statement of the district. Here are two examples of how this works (GLISI, 2013, p. 8):

School Vision Statement	District Vision Statement
[Our middle school] will be world class with students who achieve excellence in all areas. Staff will be experts in their field who are dedicated to life-long learning and student success. Families will partner with staff to help students achieve their maximum potential; and students will constantly strive to improve in everything they do.	[Our district] will become a system of world-class schools where students acquire the knowledge and skills to be successful as they continue their education at the postsecondary level and/or enter the workforce.

(continued)

School Vision Statement	District Vision Statement
We, the [elementary school] community … will establish a safe and supportive environment that will maximize the potential of all students. We will provide differentiated learning experiences through authentic, engaging, and challenging instructional practices based on individual learning styles. As a family, we will foster success for all students in order to promote college and career readiness, as well as equip students with skills needed for life in the 21st century.	[Our district] provides all students the best education available anywhere, preparing every child to lead a rich and productive life.

SEE IT IN ACTION: VISION 🎞

Two detailed video examples of principals who have set visions and used them as the basis for schoolwide reform may be found at http://bit.ly/highpayoff1.

Here you will follow two principals have been developed by Public Broadcasting Service affiliate, WNET. They have set visions for their schools and how the schools reflect those aspirations. Each principal (one in New York City and the other in Gwinnett County, Georgia) has created a vision statement using stakeholder feedback and a needs assessment. The schools have recently undergone demographic changes that have required a revisioning, which the principals describe. The principals communicate the vision and are able to successfully transmit it, and they demonstrate how they have used the vision to drive instructional improvements.

Both schools use their visions to put out there what the school stands for and how it goes about delivering on this vision on a daily basis. The New York City high school principal describes how his school developed a vision for all students to be prepared for college. He describes the vision as "spirited" in that all members of the school community buy-in to it, including how it manifests itself by teachers in their classroom. The vision was created by all members of the community and involved much re-writing and refining. The vision translates into high expectations in the classrooms and all aspects of school life. Both schools in the video provide examples of putting a strong instructional focus in their visions. So, even though they are different school levels in different parts of the country, the communication of instructional focus through the vision is clear in these examples.

SHARPENING FOCUS

Of course, a vision statement needs to be implemented in all aspects of community life. All might agree that selecting a priority and devoting time and attention to it is important, but it is also insufficient. Good intentions will not make this happen. The leader has to walk the talk, infuse all efforts with the pursuit of this priority, and devote time and resources to its achievement. Coaches often refer to this as "keeping your eye on the ball." An elementary school principal has observed that "making sure that the majority of time is spent on instructional leadership is really the key to being a successful leader."

It is also worth noting that the district or school leader needs to enable others to have the same degree of time and focus in the school or district.

One principal was pleased that the leadership team successfully implemented a new system of classroom walkthroughs and coaching for teachers. As a result of this success, he thought they would be eager to engage in the development of new curriculum. Instead, he encountered resistance. What was going to be taken off their plate so they could concentrate on this new work? If it was just an add-on, not only did it seem less important but also they did not have the time to focus on this new work. What's good for the principal is good for the team!

FOCUS FACTORS

In addition to paying careful attention, there are at least four important focus factors:

- Engage personally.

  Leaders must always walk the talk. They must transparently devote time and energy to the priority strategy and communicate often about its progress to the larger community. From a symbolic perspective, leaders should become the embodiment of the priority. When stakeholders see leaders, they should be reminded of this strategy and ask how it's going.

- Share leadership.

  We already know that leaders cannot get results working on their own. This is important for the leader's focus in two ways: it is crucial to have a leadership team and others who share the vision and undertake activities to bring it about. It is equally important that others are asked to perform tasks that free up time for the leader so he or she can concentrate on the priority.

- Align all resources: money, people, and time.

  Resources are always finite. How they are allocated should be the leader's purposeful decision. Rethinking the leader's time, assignments of talented staff, and use of funding requires purposeful planning and the political will to make hard decisions that will focus these resources on the achievement of the strategy even if they disturb the status quo. Principals who have been successful, for example, have coaches to work with teachers in an ongoing way. Where do they get this funding? Do they just have a larger budget than their colleagues? Unlikely. They understand the importance of coaches as support for teachers and reallocate funding to ensure that these positions exist.

- Know the numbers.

  As with any change effort, a baseline must be identified so any assessment of subsequent progress can be measured. Even the most effective leaders often underestimate their starting point. For example, when principals begin their participation in the National SAM [school administration manager] Innovation Program (NSIP, a nationwide program that helps school and district leaders analyze their use of time in order to gain more time for the leader to concentrate on instructional improvements), they are asked to estimate what percentage of their time is used to lead instruction. Almost always they overestimate. They usually think they spend about 75 percent of their time focused on instruction, but when they are shadowed for a week, the data almost always reveal that it is closer to 25 percent. Armed with these data and a variety of tools and coaching, participants are able to focus their time on improving instruction — often within a few months.

See It in Action: Sharpening Focus 📹

Two detailed examples of principals have been developed by Public Broadcasting Service affiliate, WNET. They may be found at http://bit.ly/highpayoff2.

The principals in this video use different techniques to align their use of time with the instructional priorities they have set. They use various processes and staff to protect their time from distractions so they can concentrate on leading instruction. Among the techniques they use are delegation, shared leadership, and data analysis.

The principal from Gwinnett County uses the SAM process referenced previously in this chapter. This includes daily consultation with the SAM to determine the schedule for the day in ways that prioritize the principal's time on instruction and delegate other responsibilities and identification of first responders who handle matters before they reach the principal's desk. We also hear from a teacher in the school who describes how the principal now has the time to discuss lessons with him and uses time effectively for coaching.

The two schools in these videos have different approaches to "protecting the time" of the principal. We see one principal focus her time on instruction through delegating tasks to teacher teams, attendance team, and the coaches team. There is a "pipeline" where everyone knows where to go to get problems solved. The principal also uses her cabinet to plan her daily schedule. The second school uses the National SAMs Innovation Program. The principal uses his assistant as his "SAM" (School Administration Manager). She helps him set goals and sees that the school runs well and that the principal is always informed without having to be personally involved with every decision.

WHAT CAN GET IN THE WAY?

Maintaining focus can be difficult because education leaders' jobs are demanding and busy. Time management experts often refer to the leader's job as a "series of interruptions interrupted by other interruptions." This is not far from the mark. Nevertheless, if the leader knows what is likely to get in the way, plans can be made to overcome these potential derailers.

- The inability to say that one strategy is more important than others

  This obstacle is more pronounced for education leaders than leaders in many other sectors because they have a mission to improve life for generations of students and clearly *everything* that contributes to that is important and must receive attention. Right? That is the surest route to both a nervous breakdown and a lack of accomplishment. It is of utmost importance that the leader is able to set priorities and persist in the attention to these.

- The inability to let go

  Leaders often believe that they have to handle everything personally. One of the hardest parts of being an effective leader is letting go. It is the leader's job to define the priorities (with lots of input), develop the plan and milestones (with lots of input), and develop the teams that will take the work forward. At that point, the leader must share the leadership and let go. Everything will not be done exactly as it would had the leader personally performed all the tasks, but the bottom line will be achieved and there will be more buy-in as well.

- Crisis management

Time gets out of hand as the day moves forward. Even with the best intentions and plans at the beginning of the day, urgent matters arise and the leader moves from one crisis to another. Some really require the leader's immediate attention, but most can be handled by others. One of the findings of NSIP (as leaders delegate non-instructional work to others and spend their time on instruction) has been that it's hard to break the habit of handling crises. There is a shorter term sense of satisfaction about having been able to solve a crisis than the harder, deeper dive into the longer-term instructional focus.

- Resistance from others who now have to handle the non-instructional tasks

What about resistance that might be felt by others as the leader spends more time on instruction? The resistance is mitigated if there is a strong value for instruction in the school, and therefore it would make sense that leaders would put their focus there. However, those who have to deal with more non-instructional issues may not be pleased.

Here's how one assistant principal (AP) successfully handled this.

As this AP spent more time on instructional issues, teachers felt that he was ignoring their needs regarding student behavior issues. The AP made a smart adjustment to his procedure that combined both instruction and student behavior issues. Instead of calling unruly students to his office, he went to see them in their classrooms. This gave him the additional time he wanted to visit classrooms, where he was able to address real-time behavior issues and also prevent future such issues because he was so visible. One teacher remarked, "Wow, you should have been doing this a long time ago!" Everyone felt supported, and the AP was able to keep his focus on instruction.

MAINTAINING FOCUS: IMPLICATIONS FOR THE HIGH-PAYOFF STRATEGIES

A crucial part of achieving the high-payoff strategy is to keep a sharp focus. This attribute cuts across all three high-payoff strategies. For example, if you want to create a supportive culture, the organization's values will have to be intentionally incorporated in all aspects of what goes on. For any new priority pursued, it must be obvious how it furthers the existing values.

If curriculum and pedagogic improvements are sought, it must be clear that instruction is the priority and, even though there are many other ongoing activities, the leader's attention is focused squarely on instruction and others are assigned leadership roles in other areas. Funding will be reallocated so that instructional coaches can be hired to work with teachers on this priority area. Teacher leaders will receive professional development (in and out of school) to support their efforts in this priority area.

Leaders must allocate ongoing support and additional time to facilitate learning communities. Other supports for expert consultation or supplies and materials, as identified by the participants, also need to be a priority.

A SELF-REFLECTIVE TOOL FOR LEADER VISION AND FOCUS

This chapter closes with a short tool for leaders to use to guide them in incorporating techniques that will help sharpen their focus on the priority areas. Then we're on to the specific exploration of the three high-payoff strategies.

SELF-REFLECTION ON VISION AND FOCUS

Part One: We have the following inspirational and aspirational vision:

_____

_____

_____

_____

Part Two: Here is the high-payoff strategy I intend to pursue:

_____

_____

_____

_____

The Scale: Indicate the extent to which you demonstrate each focus factor by using the five-point scale: 5 = always, 4 = often, 3 = sometimes, 2 = infrequently, 1 = never. The higher your score, the more focused you are. This exercise will help you to identify where you can improve.

To what extent do I do the following?

FOCUS FACTOR	RATING	EXAMPLE
I. Personally Engage		
a. Always pay attention to what is going on related to this strategy	5 4 3 2 1	
b. Am immediately responsive to time-sensitive matters that come up regarding the strategy, even if I am busy	5 4 3 2 1	
c. Communicate my personal commitment and enthusiasm for the strategy in almost everything I do	5 4 3 2 1	
II. Share Leadership		
a. Develop a leadership team that shares the priority of the strategy	5 4 3 2 1	
b. Identify first responders for all non-strategy-related activities to be the first point of contact on such matters (even if they ultimately bring the issue to me)	5 4 3 2 1	
III. Align Resources		
a. Devote the time necessary for the accomplishment of the strategy (re-allocate time from other activities)	5 4 3 2 1	
b. Have the members of the leadership team (and others) share leadership for the priority	5 4 3 2 1	
c. Allocate financial resources to the accomplishment of the strategy (reallocate existing resources; secure new ones)	5 4 3 2 1	
IV. Know the Numbers		
a. Keep track through ongoing use of data how I'm doing on all the above	5 4 3 2 1	

SUMMARY

Areas of strength:

_____

_____

_____

_____

Areas for development:

Part 1

Strategy: Culture

Chapter 3

Creating a Culture Supportive of Teaching and Learning

> What I love most about being a principal is being able to shape the culture to what we all want it to be.
>
> —A suburban high school principal

It's easy to tell when you've entered a school with great leaders. You don't see students congregating on the street or loitering in the hallway, yet you hear their voices drifting from classrooms. Signs in the entranceway welcome you to the school and proclaim the principal's vision for the school community. Perhaps a first floor bulletin board contains the principal's goals for herself and for the students, has a message from the head of the parents' association, and displays honors achieved by the school in the past.

There might be a countdown clock that displays the number of books read by the school's students so far this year toward the goal of twenty-five each, with covers of those finished artistically displayed.

Other bulletin boards are filled with the work of students arrayed by projects done in their class, with descriptions by their teacher of the lesson that resulted in these products. As you sign in, the security guard volunteers, "Oh, you're here to see Ms. Smith. You're going to love her. We all do; she's made such a difference here."

As you walk to the main office, many teachers have their classroom doors open (hence the audibility of student voices). Bulletin boards near the main office display data on student attendance: attendance rates by grade level, by class, and the names of those students with perfect attendance.

Once you get to the main office, you are greeted by the principal's assistant, who invites you to have a seat. The principal is not in the office and probably will not return for a while. She is visiting the classrooms of teachers and having discussions with them about their lessons. Of course you understand. This principal has a laser focus on instruction that is evident throughout the school.

You also know when you've entered a district office where teaching children is the pervasive value. In fact, you get that point even before you've set foot into the building. Take the offices of Gwinnett County Public Schools, for example. This district office is called the "Instructional Support Center," which is proclaimed not only on the building itself but also on the highway and traffic signs that lead to this destination. The naming of the building and the signs along the way reflect the district culture as led by the superintendent. He repeats the message in all he does.

Great schools and districts have highly held shared values; they have common expectations for adults and students that are observable through artifacts, language, ceremonies, rituals, shared history, and symbols. In other words—culture. In fact, there are several cultures operating at any given time. There is a district culture, a school culture, a department culture, a community culture—even a different culture in every classroom. This forms the backdrop of everything that happens.

Culture represents a shared-meaning perspective or way of interpreting events. It is the way things are done around here, a cocoon that makes everyone feel safe and belonging. This is why culture can be comforting and used for stability when other changes are contemplated. People are reassured that the bottom line, their values, is not threatened even though other changes may be afoot. It is both bottom-up and leader-influenced.

USE OF SYMBOLS

Symbols are important when understanding culture. There is meaning in what you can see. Everything discussed at the beginning of this chapter is a symbol—student work on the bulletin boards, open classroom doors, and attendance data. This tells quite a lot about the way things are done.

Use of symbols is, therefore, not only a good way to see the culture but also for leaders to change the culture. One principal, who wanted to encourage teachers to use data more frequently, set up a data room with data maps. Not only was this a useful resource but also it was a strong symbol of the importance of data. And, as it was used more and more, data became a way of life in the school.

Of course, the principal is a symbol of the culture by nature of the position. What image does the principal want to portray? This should be a conscious choice.

Take the elementary school principal in North Carolina who was unhappy that the students looked at her as a disciplinarian. As is the case with many principals, it was not looked on favorably to be called to the principal's office, but this particular principal did not want herself or the administration to be perceived in this way. She wanted to be a symbol of support for students. It was an easy, inexpensive—yet symbolic—fix.

This leader had pencils printed with the message, "I received this pencil from my principal." Students got a pencil for accomplishments—both academic and behavioral. Before long, students clamored to be called to the principal's office to be awarded a pencil, which they used with pride. And the image of the principal in the school's culture changed dramatically.

SHARED VALUES

There are certain values that are found in high-achieving schools and districts. We'll call them *instruction-centered values*. Effective leaders know and build on the values of the members, but they also lead the organization to elevate certain values to prominence.

But all culture isn't observable. It is also what people *believe*—both what they say, but more important, how they behave (which may be different and is always more real). Culture also includes common assumptions that are just there for everyone in the group—beliefs so deeply held that they are below the surface and taken as fact or reality by group members—unless and until they are challenged or explored.

The keen observer of culture will recognize behaviors as indicative of shared values, that is, what people believe is reflected in their day-to-day actions. Even though people don't often talk about their values, these can be seen in their actions.

Of course, each group has its own culture. Each school, each district, and each professional association—even each classroom has its own culture. People belong to several groups with distinctive cultures, but in education organizations there are usually values that are common across the board. The effective leader identifies these and builds on them. High-functioning schools and districts develop cultures that support the learning of all involved with the education of the community members.

The friendly warning here is that culture is always in play. As one middle school principal put it, "We didn't seek improvement in culture. Culture sought us out. It found us." So ignore culture at your peril. Take charge of leading culture change and you will set the stage for everything else needed to achieve the vision.

Cultures develop in two simultaneous ways: they reflect the cumulative real values of community members and also show the clear instruction-centered values driven by the leaders. A culture needs to be built on high expectations for students and the adults. Learning is job one for everyone: the principal and other school leaders, parents and other partners, district leaders, teachers and students. Sometimes these values are one and the same—but often they are not. It is the leaders' job to build an instructionally focused culture. Learning organizations are not only for the students. The goal is continual improvement. Everyone is capable of high achievement.

SHARED VALUES AS SYMBOLS

In addition to the foundational belief that all students are capable of high achievement, the culture values respect for everyone as demonstrated by openness, candor, and trust. Students and adults alike are acknowledged and recognized for their contributions as well as for their efforts, even if sometimes they are unsuccessful. Learning from mistakes is a goal and in this way risk taking is valued and leads to new ways of approaching issues that arise and to support constant learning and improving. And, of course, using data to inform decisions is important.

The following examples show how this can work.

An elementary school in Maryland proudly displays its values on a wall posting at the school's entrance and on all school stationary. It is integrated into all facets of school life: PRIDE, which stands for "positive attitude, respect, integrity, discovery, excellence."

The superintendent of a western district has led a process with all instructional staff to discuss the importance of shared values and to jointly choose which core values the district should focus on. Further, the shared values are clearly described as to what they look like in action. All district documents show them:

1. Students First—We put our kids' needs at the forefront of everything we do.
2. Integrity—We tell the truth and we keep our promises.
3. Equity—We celebrate diversity and will provide the necessary resources and supports to eliminate barriers.
4. Collaboration—Together as a team, we think, we work, and we create in order to reach our goals.
5. Accountability—We take responsibility for our individual and collective commitments.
6. Fun—We celebrate the joy in our work and foster in our students a joy and passion for learning.

Let's consider how the building blocks described in chapter 1 apply to the building of culture: getting buy-in, starting with an early win, and providing ongoing support.

GETTING BUY-IN: "WE'RE ALL IN THIS TOGETHER"

There is no better way to get people's buy-in to a shared culture than to find out about the individual values of each group member—preferably from each of them personally. People express those values in the context of their roles in the district or school, which is essential to their satisfaction and ability to function effectively. Personal values are important because people don't leave their values on the doorstep as they enter headquarters or the school. Getting this information is easy.

Talk with people; survey them, conduct focus groups, or, as advised in this book, conduct an exercise to measure the culture. It may seem daunting to try to get individual input from a large number of faculty members. It isn't. Conducting the measuring-the-culture exercise can be accomplished in thirty to forty minutes. All staff members will have a personal experience that helps them clarify their own values and see how their values mesh with those of the school's culture.

One problem is an unproductive, principal-driven culture. That is to say, if something does not come from the principal, it won't be done. The most effective cultures are shared. School community members will buy into the overall culture if they contribute to building it. Some if not most of each person's values will be shared by most community members. As buy-in is achieved by finding out about shared values, the leader can attempt to also get buy-in for instruction-centered values, which might not currently be apparent.

STARTING WITH AN EARLY WIN

The commitment to putting highly held values into action can be a good early win. This could come as the publicizing of a values statement for the school that incorporates the shared values (now that you know what they are). Similar to the previously discussed elementary school's PRIDE motto, this is an important symbol of commitment—and also tests the assumption of whether the words chosen are indeed the values.

In that western district, they celebrated an early win once the educators had chosen the shared values. They called it "Values Day," and everyone from the district came together (school leaders, central office staff, teachers, secretaries, bus drivers, parents, lunchroom workers, custodians) to celebrate and reflect on the shared core values and make a personal connection to the vision. It was a day dedicated to developing a common understanding of how to put the core values into action at all places in the school system. Having established this as an early win, it is now an annual occurrence.

> Another example: A suburban elementary school principal wanted to change the school culture from one that used little data and employed a one-size-fits-all approach to instruction to a culture in which ongoing, formative assessment was used to identify individual student needs. Teachers did not value this data-informed approach. As an early win, the principal scheduled individual meetings with each teacher to talk about the data for the students in that teacher's class. Although teachers did not initially value data, they *did* value recognition and coaching from the principal. They were pleased to get this individual attention. Once the principal had their attention, she was able to demonstrate how useful it was to review the data and incorporate what was learned into teachers' lessons.

A different type of early win is to choose one widely held value, develop a plan to get more of it into daily life, and report back on how it goes. For example, in several schools, teachers use the measuring-the-culture exercise with their students. This gives the students the same experience that their teachers had, providing data for teachers to use as motivation in lesson plans, and symbolizes the importance of learning for all community members. After that early win, do the same with other widely held values.

PROVIDING ONGOING SUPPORT

Knowing members' values and aspiring to the instruction-centered values is necessary but not sufficient. There must be constant emphasis and support for these values so they are expressed in all facets of the organization's daily life. This means that members' values and the aspirational instruction-centered values must be on display and in use constantly. This isn't as hard as it might seem.

People's values are very important to them. They will flood you with ideas of how to incorporate them more into daily life. Just ask! You can even put parameters around the acceptable ideas, such as they can't involve additional funding. It doesn't matter. People who hold these values will have many ideas. Ongoing support involves putting those ideas into action.

> For example, staff members in one district office valued teaching and learning but found themselves far from the action. They suggested, and the superintendent agreed, to go in teams each month to other schools to observe personally the effects of various policies of the district office on teaching and learning in the schools. They spoke with teachers, observed classrooms, and debriefed the experiences with the leadership team. It wouldn't surprise readers to learn that this on-the-ground perspective led to changes in district policies—making them less cumbersome and more supportive of teaching and learning.

SEE IT IN ACTION: LEADING SCHOOL CULTURE 🎬

Two detailed examples of principals who have developed innovative ways to build the school's culture – or climate" follow with have been developed by Public Broadcasting Service affiliate WNET. They may be found at http://bit.ly/highpayoff3.

In the video the two principals discuss the relationship between school culture and academic performance. They have led school culture in ways that create a supportive climate for teaching and learning—through systems and processes that are observable. They have aligned the culture experienced by the students with the larger school culture experienced by the adults. We also see the manifestation of the culture in the shared leadership the principals employ—in which the values of the school are seen in other leaders. Also observable is the importance of parental involvement in furthering the community culture of the school.

The middle school in Prince George's County, Maryland demonstrates how culture can be used to take a school from one with student behavior problems that are getting in the way of instruction to one where there is consistency of expectation across all the adults and students in the building. Culture change has led to cutting student suspensions by 90% and an openness and sharing among teachers and among teachers and administration. This culture change was brought about by having a Culture Responsiveness Task Force comprised of a cross-section of folks. Some practices it led to are the creation of a new position, Assistant Principal of Culture, celebration of student success, and student uniforms. Consistency was the goal. And it was achieved.

> The Bronx, New York elementary school also featured in the video shows how the culture was transformed by emphasizing a preventative approach whereby each student's learning needs were diagnosed with data. The video also shows the school's "Positive Behavior Intervention and Support" initiative, whereby students who succeed are able to make purchases from the store. Finally, teachers now visit and observe each other—and offer feedback in collegial ways—using an open culture to improve the basis for teaching and learning.

WHAT CAN GET IN THE WAY?

Establishing a culture that is supportive of teaching and learning is essential but hard to do. Here are some reasons why.

Culture Is Often Invisible

Mistakes can be made if the culture is inadvertently upset. We know that happens all the time. Why? Because some of the most important aspects of the culture are assumptions that members carry with them. They are so ingrained that people just assume they are reality. And this refers not only to huge assumptions such as worldviews but also to small things that have resulted from shared history within the organization.

Just ask the new teacher on her first day who poured out the hot water she took from the watercooler on deciding that she didn't want tea after all. Those in the break room were clearly miffed. The new teacher had inadvertently stumbled into culture, in this case, history. The watercooler was hard won last year, and to pour out the water was disrespectful to the effort that had gone into getting it. It was an inauspicious beginning for that teacher's relationship with her colleagues. Who knew?

People Don't Know Their Own Values

Because people's values are so important to them, one would think that everyone would be aware of them all the time—in fact, they would live by them. If only this were so! It is true that those who are most fulfilled live a life in which they always act in accordance with their values; this is not usually the case. When we form our values, in our youth mostly, we give a lot of thought to this. However, once we enter the world, have chosen careers, and establish family life, for most of us, thinking about our values recedes into the background. Been there, done that.

However, our values often change as our life experience does. Seldom do we take the time to reflect on how our values have changed until there is some sort of dilemma or crisis that leads us to wonder if there is some gap between what we value and how we are living our lives. Often our values are more clearly observable to *others* than to ourselves. Others who interact with us and watch our behavior are often more aware than we are of what we think is important.

In reality, most people grow and change their values (or at least the order of their priority in their lives). As we become more satisfied with the presence of a value in our lives, we sometimes take it for granted, and achieving another value becomes a higher priority. We don't stop to recognize this, but we behave in different ways.

Valuing health is a good example. Most people take health for granted when they are healthy. If something happens to question their health (or the health of someone close to them), health as a value becomes a top priority.

In one middle school, the teachers didn't realize how much they valued professional development until a scheduling conflict prevented sessions from taking place one semester. They missed the knowledge, comradery, and social interaction—and prevailed on the principal to change the schedule back—restoring those sessions that previously had been taken for granted.

The Leader Makes Assumptions

Leaders are human beings. They also have personal values and need to be reflective of those and how they may have changed. However, it is essential that leaders realize that their personal values are just that—their *own* personal values. Those values are not indicative of what is important to anyone else. We all tend to think that what we value is automatically shared by others. It's our way of interpreting the world. But this isn't the case. Not testing these assumptions leads to a misinterpretation of the culture. Therefore, once leaders reflect on their own values, they then must put those aside and objectively help others critically analyze theirs.

A similar obstacle is that leaders sometimes make untested assumptions about the values of others. This often comes about by the leader observing the behaviors of others and adding an interpretation rather than finding out what is really going on. For example, an elementary school principal lamented that the teachers "just didn't value professional development." This was very disappointing to her and also disruptive of her plans to improve instruction in the school.

On what evidence did this principal base her view that teachers did not value professional development? During the sessions, many teachers were distracted, checked their watches often, and ran out immediately when the session concluded. The leader interpreted that they "clearly" weren't interested. However, this wasn't the case. Professional development was important to the teachers. However, the sessions were scheduled at the end of the day—when many teachers had to pick up their children from daycare or after-school programs. The priority value was their children. This didn't mean, however, that they didn't also value professional development.

Values aren't absolute; they are relative. Something can be important, but something else can be *more so.*

Once the principal tested this assumption and found out what was really going on, she found a better time to schedule professional development. Once the conflict was resolved between the two values (learning and family), both were accommodated and professional development was well received.

People Misunderstand the Importance of Symbols

The symbolic aspect of culture is very important. It is a public display of mission, appreciation, and what is valued. This is the reason, for example, that salary, raises, and bonuses are often more important as symbols of achievement or appreciation than the actual purchasing power of the money. It is of great importance that, if something is a symbol of a larger message, it is not changed unless the leader means to send a message that what was represented by the symbol is no longer valued.

Here's something that illustrates this point: it was a long-established practice in the district office that, when it was your birthday, everyone gathered in the conference room at 3:00 to "surprise" you with a birthday cake. Of course, it was no surprise. You anticipated it, looked forward to it, and probably even dressed up for it that day.

Enter a new administration. Scouring the budget for cost-savings, they found the annual $400 spent on birthday cakes and removed it. An easy enough line item saving, right? Wrong. The birthday cake wasn't a birthday cake. It was a symbol of appreciation of staff members' hard work and contribution because you were recognized by your colleagues on your special day. It was also a symbol of the family atmosphere in the district.

To save an annual $400, morale plummeted. For days, the absence of birthday cake celebrations was all that anyone talked about. People were so unhappy with how the culture had been disrupted that they chipped in themselves to restore the celebration. This actually proved how much the cake and celebration were symbols of the enduring culture. But, the new leader caused much disruption by not understanding the importance of this symbol—and didn't even save money because the time wasted by people's ruminations about this issue was clearly more expensive.

Knowing what can get in the way helps to avoid the pitfalls. The measuring-the-culture tool that follows should help leaders develop the supportive culture and get the buy-in and needed data to develop the early win and ongoing support.

Chapter 4

Using Data to Plan Culture Strategies

Because culture can be hidden, testing its assumptions is a must for any leader. In order to identify the more hidden aspects of the culture, the leader needs to know what values are most prevalent. Are there some values that are of higher priority than others to the majority of adults? That is usually the case and is very important to know. How many people hold which values? Of the instruction-centered values, which are present to a large degree? Which need to be pursued? It is also important to know which of the instruction-centered values are shared (so those may be enhanced) and which are not yet strongly on the radar so strategies can be made to help inculcate them. In this way, the values of those who work there can be furthered, leading to increased satisfaction.

In addition, the leader can identify values that are missing for the type of culture necessary to drive needed changes. The leader can therefore begin with making sure most community members identify their values in daily life and find some that are instruction centered to move forward. As people become comfortable with the culture, the leader can introduce additional instruction-centered values that might not be at the top of everyone's list—and slowly integrate them into the culture.

Administration of the exercise in this chapter provides the leader with the data needed to plan the high-payoff culture strategy described in chapter 3 because it surveys all the teachers and leaders in the school or district. It assesses which of the instruction-centered values are present and which are not. It promotes buy-in by providing a personal experience for each participant (even if there are hundreds of them) and helps plan an early win. Further, it provides the basis for determining what ongoing support is needed to sustain and further the early win. The values identified will be real because this exercise facilitates people to examine their own values closely.

This chapter presents the exercise, instructions for its administration (a leader's guide), and ideas for how to use the resulting data to plan a high-payoff culture strategy.

THE MEASURING-THE-CULTURE EXERCISE

From this half-hour exercise, the leader will get a compilation of the highest held values of each participant, making a distinction between each person's number one value and the rest of his or her top five. The leader will also be able to analyze any discrepancies between the needed instruction-focused culture and the shared values of the school community.

> The principal of a rural K–8 school in Kentucky provided the following commentary after conducting the measuring the culture exercise for the teachers at his school:
>
> We conducted the session last night and were amazed at the great discussion and the priorities of the faculty. We approached the [session] from two strands: (1) we wanted to understand the faculty's priority goals and, in turn, we wanted teachers to conduct the same session with their students to get to know them better. I developed a PowerPoint from the leader's guide and found some video clips that were appropriate to use in introducing and closing the session. We used the dramatics and had a wastebasket that we had participants come up and throw their values away. I also used color-coded index cards so we could distinguish elementary from middle school teachers.
>
> You should have heard the discussion. At first they thought it was going to be easy, but realized how hard it really was as we went along. All of the faculty had some surprises and struggled most with narrowing their top ten when they figured in the [evidence].
>
> I am creating a spreadsheet with the results of the tallies and then sharing it with the faculty. I am now going to use the results to have them develop strategies to motivate the teachers. The teachers, even the primary teachers, want to use this [exercise] with their students. They will simplify for primary, but are really interested in learning about their children's values. One of the biggest surprises was that some were unsure of what a few of the values were and so we had some great discussion around the values themselves. This was very worthwhile to the faculty and to me.
>
> A leader of in mid-Atlantic district similarly has called the measuring-the-culture experience powerful and is using it with all leaders in the district in order to plan an instructional-centered culture for all schools and the district office.

Here's the handout for each participant.

The Measuring-the-Culture Exercise

What is most important?	10 Highest (X)	Circle Extent Valued (5 = Highest; 1 = Lowest)	5 Highest (X)
		Column A + Column B = Column C	
Being in control		5 4 3 2 1	
Being liked		5 4 3 2 1	
Candor		5 4 3 2 1	
Celebration		5 4 3 2 1	
Change		5 4 3 2 1	
Competition		5 4 3 2 1	
Courage		5 4 3 2 1	
Creativity		5 4 3 2 1	
Data-informed decision making		5 4 3 2 1	
Diversity		5 4 3 2 1	
Empathy		5 4 3 2 1	
Financial security		5 4 3 2 1	
Fairness and equity		5 4 3 2 1	
Family life		5 4 3 2 1	
Flexibility		5 4 3 2 1	
Freedom		5 4 3 2 1	
Friendly environment		5 4 3 2 1	
Friendship		5 4 3 2 1	
Fun		5 4 3 2 1	
Health		5 4 3 2 1	
Helpfulness		5 4 3 2 1	
Hopefulness (optimism)		5 4 3 2 1	
Independence (autonomy)		5 4 3 2 1	
Integrity		5 4 3 2 1	
Job satisfaction		5 4 3 2 1	
Knowledge		5 4 3 2 1	
Leaving a legacy		5 4 3 2 1	
Love		5 4 3 2 1	
Loyalty		5 4 3 2 1	
Making a difference		5 4 3 2 1	

(continued)

What is most important?	10 Highest (X)	Circle Extent Valued (5 = Highest; 1 = Lowest)	5 Highest (X)
Meeting commitments		5 4 3 2 1	
Openness to new ideas		5 4 3 2 1	
Order and stability		5 4 3 2 1	
Perseverance		5 4 3 2 1	
Professional development		5 4 3 2 1	
Recognition		5 4 3 2 1	
Religion		5 4 3 2 1	
Spirituality		5 4 3 2 1	
Student success		5 4 3 2 1	
Respect for others		5 4 3 2 1	
Risk taking		5 4 3 2 1	
Self-respect		5 4 3 2 1	
Sharing with others		5 4 3 2 1	
Stability		5 4 3 2 1	
Trust		5 4 3 2 1	
Teamwork		5 4 3 2 1	
Wealth		5 4 3 2 1	
Work-life balance		5 4 3 2 1	

A Leader's Guide for Conducting the Exercise (Thirty to Forty Minutes)

This exercise can be conducted in a large, medium, or small group. You just need to make slight modifications for a large group as indicated in the instructions that follow.

Step One: Introduction (Three to Five Minutes)

Distribute the list of values. Ask participants to follow along with your instructions and not to try to go ahead of you or guess what comes next. Ask participants to read the list of values. Tell participants that they may add any values not on the list that they feel are important to them.

Possible optional, interesting discussion questions at this point include the following. You might want to use one or more of these questions to stimulate some discussion to set the stage in advance of the exercise.

- Ask what a *value* is and why it is so important for us to be aware of our values. Why is it important for our instructor to be aware of our values?

- Ask the definition of terms for all or for those that might prove troublesome.

- Ask what an *assumption* is and why we should always test assumptions and not just think that everyone thinks the same way we do or has the same values we do.

Step Two: Rating the Values Intuitively (Five Minutes)

1. Participants should read all the values first and then check off the ten that are the most important to them. They may use whatever intuitive methods of analysis they want to make their decisions. There are no right or wrong answers. They will not be judged on their responses. These are individual decisions.

2. When considering these values, they should consider their importance to them personally, not as an organization member. You do not leave your values at the door when you enter the building.

Facilitation tips:

1. They have only five minutes for this task (it should be off the top of their heads, without a lot of thought).

2. Warn the group when there are two minutes remaining and then when there is one minute left.

Step Three: Rating the Values on a Scale (Ten Minutes)

For each value considered, participants should provide an example of why it is important to them. In many cases this will also help clarify choices. If I have x value, it automatically includes y value, too (of course, this is an individual interpretation).

Step Four (5 minutes)

Ask participants to examine their ratings and decide upon their 5 highest values.

Step Five: The Simulation (Ten Minutes)

Give participants six index cards each, telling them to put the sixth card in a safe place to use later. On each of the five cards, they should write one of their five highest values.

Tell them they should look over the five cards and make a decision regarding which of the five cards they are most willing to give to you. In other words, which of the five is the least important of the five? Then walk around to each person and take the card that holds his or her highest value. This evokes lots of emotion as people are "giving away" their highest held values. There is much nervous laughter in the room.

Facilitation tips:

1. If you have a large group, ask participants to pass the value they are giving away to their right and you collect them from the person on the aisle.

2. It is a dramatic touch to have a clean wastebasket in which you can "discard" the values. However, you will want to keep the cards in order

to add up the total number of times a value appeared in everyone's top five, so make sure the basket is clean so you can retrieve them. Before you throw away the number five value, read them to the group. "Here is what you have given away ..." This always gets a big reaction as people experience having given away significant parts of them.

Do this three more times. People give up another value (number four); you read them and throw them away. Then do the same with the number three and number two values.

People are left with their most dearly held value. They get to keep this one. (Say, "Think of everything you had to give up in order to keep this one. It must be of incredible significance to you.")

Note: You may be tempted to skip this part of the exercise. Please do not. It is the simulation of throwing away values that brings them into critical consciousness—people are likely not aware of their own values and, if just asked to list them, would not get them right!

Step Six: Number Ones (Three Minutes)

Ask participants to retrieve the sixth index card. On this card they are to make a copy of their number one value to hand to you for counting. They should write the value on the card and "#1." Point out that you are *not taking this away from them*. That is why you gave them the sixth card.

Read out the number one responses. Point out how important they are. Tell the participants to think of what they had to give up in order to keep this one. It is very significant to their motivation and life choices.

Note: Be careful about asking people to share their values with the group. Some people will want to do this and others will not. No one should share his or her values if they do not want to do this. But if they do, it can be a very interesting discussion.

Step Seven: Restoring the Values (Two Minutes)

People will feel stripped of important parts of themselves. You should have a little ceremony. Raise your hands and pronounce, "By the authority vested in me as the instructor of this class, I hereby restore to you the values I took away." Everyone will laugh and feel better.

Step Eight: Discussion Questions (If There Is Time)

- Which was the hardest value for you to give up? The first one? The last one? Why?

- Were you surprised with the value you kept as number one? Is it one you might have predicted?

- Did you have any values in your top five that weren't even in your original top ten? In other words, values that only became apparent to you after you examined additional perspectives?

- Do you think these were your values at other points in your life? Might they change at other points in your life?

Step Nine: Follow-Up: Compiling and Analyzing the Results (May Be Done Virtually or at the Next Meeting)

Count the cards given away and you'll get the number of each value that was in the participants' top five values. Keep track of the number one values separately. You get a composite of the values of this group and consequently its culture now that participants have critically analyzed their values for their appropriateness in their lives today.

Optional: You might ask participants to hand in anonymously their scaled scores. If you have these, you can calculate schoolwide averages for each value (instead of knowing only the top five). You would know which values are low across the board—which you won't know from just collecting the cards (some might be high, just not as high as the top five). You will gain a lot from knowing if there is actual resistance to some of the values that are needed for instructional focus.

And, a final note about personal values versus those more evident in school. People do not leave their personal values at the doorstep when then come to work. If personal values—such as family life and health—are more important than school values (such as student success), you need to know this. And, those who hold these values will be able to suggest how to translate them into productive values for the school. Family life might translate into annual family outings for school community members or even treating colleagues as family—holding social gatherings or even team meetings.

Here's a summary template you might use.

Culture Analyses: (n = XX)

Value	Number or Percentage Cited as Number One	Number or Percentage Cited in Top Five

Here's an example of the data from one elementary school.

Culture Analysis: (n = 35)

Value	Number or Percentage Cited as Number One	Number or Percentage Cited in Top Five
Family life	11 (31%)	15 (43%)
Love	7 (31%)	24 (68%)
Student success	7 (20%)	7 (20%)
Work-life balance	4 (11%)	15 (43%)
Integrity	4 (11%)	7 (20%)
Fun	2 (6%)	7 (20%)

If I were the leader of this school, here's what I would understand from these data:

- The values are centered on relationships and warm feelings. I would do nothing to disrupt this and would ask for advice on how to get more of this into daily school life. These can further accomplish any vision.

- Student success is an important shared value — that's great for achieving the vision. But I need to understand that family life is a higher value (and more often rated number one).

- Regarding instructional-centered values, what is missing is data-informed decision making. I would look at the scaled scores (five to one ratings) to see if this was rated low or just didn't make the top five. In any case, I would know that I need to put a strategy in place to increase teachers' value for making decisions based on data.

- The number one value is family life (and work-life balance is highly rated) so I would be careful that I didn't schedule important activities that conflicted with staff members' family responsibilities. I would also make team time social and feel like family.

- I would stress collaboration over competition when planning strategies.

Here's a follow-up group discussion you might want to lead. In any case, these are the questions you might consider as you think through your high-payoff culture strategy.

Number one values

What were the number one values? These are the values that will rule the day when participants are pressed. Are the number ones clustered or individualized?

In the previous example, you would emphasize job satisfaction even though affection or love had more votes overall. Affection or love has more number ones.

Conflicts between highly held values

Analyze situations for existing values conflicts when both values are highly rated but participants are asked to choose activities of one over the other. Can you eliminate these?

Getting participants' values expressed more

Facilitate group members' brainstorming strategies to incorporate more of their values into their work (they will flood you with ideas). A question that sometimes comes up is, "What happens if the values are mostly those that are personal and not instruction-centered?" "How can we get more health in our culture, for example?" The answer is that all values count! Those that do not have an immediately apparent connection with teaching and learning actually do. And those who hold those values can tell you how they relate.

Build on the instruction-centered values to create a foundation for teaching and learning

Are the organization's values instruction-centered? How can these be emphasized more?

The leader's values don't count

Recognize that your values might not be reflective of those of the group.

Use participants' values for stability

How can the group values be used to promote stability in times of change?

Don't inadvertently upset the culture

If there are participant values that are disrespected by the existing culture — without reason — stop that practice.

Values change

Be aware that values change and sometimes can change quickly and dramatically. Do this exercise annually.

Part 2

Strategy: Instructional Improvements

Chapter 5

Leading Instructional Improvements

In this district, you are either teaching children or supporting those who do.
— A district leader

Obviously the heart of the work for district and school leaders is improving instruction for the students. As we know, they don't do this directly but through the skills, enthusiasm, and experience of those who teach children on a daily basis. So, to keep a laser focus and build a strong foundation of shared values—what do leaders actually do to effect excellent instruction for all students? The list is long and important—because the impact is district- and schoolwide.

The strategies span everything from the leader's expertise in teaching both adults and children to his or her ability to making structural changes in school schedules to enable faculty members to plan excellent instruction together. Some strategies used by effective principals include clear curricula with room for individual teacher creativity; teachers observing other teachers—in their school and in other schools; getting students' perspectives on the relevance of what they are learning to incorporate into instructional planning; reflection on instruction (assessing what is working and what isn't—continual improvement); celebrations; and structures that accommodate these activities.

School leaders work shoulder-to-shoulder with teachers to support their instructional practice. This includes the content of teaching and how the content is delivered (pedagogy). Examples include classroom walkthroughs (shorter than fifteen minutes) and observations (longer than fifteen minutes) that include discussion and coaching for the teacher; providing other coaching sessions; conducting and participating in curriculum planning meetings; conducting and participating in skills-building professional development sessions; leading the school leadership team; conducting meetings with parents regarding how they can help their children learn at home; and meeting with the superintendent, principal supervisor, and other district staff to discuss curriculum content.

Little things can be strategic. For example, instead of the good practice of personally greeting each student by name each morning as he or she walks into the building (or during their lunch), one elementary school principal always includes an instructionally specific question. So, instead of just saying, "Good morning, James," an effective principal might say "Good morning, James. What's the most interesting thing you are learning in science right now?" This is similar to the principal who always has flash cards handy when she greets students at lunch in the cafeteria. Students are always prepared to answer a quick math question. These activities don't take extra time but support the strategy of improving instruction in important ways.

> Another approach, illustrated by an elementary school in Kentucky, is to always begin faculty meetings by having teachers write reflective journals about their teaching experiences that month. The principal collects the journals and provides timely, written feedback.

Principals often get students' perspectives directly. Some hold book discussion sessions; some have lunch monthly with groups of students. At a school in Illinois, the principal often shadows a student for an entire day. Students fill out applications to be selected to be shadowed. The principals participate as that student in all lessons and activities. After the shadowing experience, the principals meet with the teachers to discuss the lessons.

Here are some examples of ways to use structure to improve instruction:

- At a middle school in Missouri, teachers in core subjects are provided with a substitute for one class period each week. They use this time to observe another teacher using a new instructional technology. Following that observation, they meet to reflect on what worked and what didn't with the principal acting as facilitator.

- In order to make sure he meets with all new teachers, a principal in Illinois schedules regular meetings with each new teacher every seven to ten days on a rotating basis. The meetings focus on instructional issues.

- At a middle school in Iowa, the principal schedules forty-five-minute sessions each week with teaching teams to work on lesson design.

Of course, district leaders can aid these efforts or thwart them. Effective district leaders develop networks of principals with whom school leaders share their successes and identify areas for improvement that they would like to learn from their colleagues. District leaders find the time to convene these sessions and often facilitate them. They identify learning needs of school leaders, bring in outside experts as needed, and provide professional development and coaching for school leaders.

Knowing what effective instruction looks like—at the school and district levels—is essential to achieving the vision. It is important to narrow the focus from "instructional improvement" to specific ways in which that plays out. Setting those as a districtwide or schoolwide goal is key—along with descriptions of what it looks like in action. Of course, a vision is only a vision unless it comes to life in the district or school.

Effective leaders shift the way teachers perceive instruction—they model, video exemplary teachers, and develop teacher leaders. They give teachers a greater voice in instructional practices.

> A middle school principal reports that she always engages in a feedback session with the teacher on the same day as an observation and then schedules a session within the next week when they can discuss the lesson more in depth.

Here are some examples of visions developed in districts and schools with effective leaders.

At a Georgia middle school, the vision is "to foster critical thinking and effective writing in every student in every classroom." Here's a summary of what this looks like in action:

In Language Arts, every student will write a minimum of one formal essay per quarter. These essays will be focused on argumentative and expository writing and will be graded on all domains (ideas, organization, fluency, and conventions) using the middle grades rubrics; and all common assessment will include one or more constructed response questions that will count as 10 percent of the assessment score.

In Math, all common assessments will include one or more constructed response questions that will count as 10 percent of the assessment score. These responses will be graded using the paragraph rubric created by the school's literacy team.

In Social Studies and Science, each student will write a minimum of one formal essay per semester. These essays should contain document-based questions asking students to write about a content-related topic using background knowledge and given documents. These essays will be graded on ideas and organization using the content area rubric created by the school's literacy team. All common assessments will include one or more constructed-response questions that will count as 20 percent of the assessment score. These responses will be graded using the paragraph rubric created by the school's literacy team.

Another elementary school principal had a vision that improving instruction was a shared responsibility between teachers and parents. The school implemented a classroom-based, parental involvement model that links school and home learning in order to increase student achievement. Parents become full partners in their child's education in their child's classrooms. Teachers value the true partnerships that are developing with parents.

A vision being sought by many schools is the use of ongoing assessments of student work via multiple methods to inform how to individualize the way they are taught going forward (formative assessment). This was the singular focus decided on by one school and everyone was devoted to its pursuit. The teachers of each grade level developed standards (learning targets) for student work and provided feedback to them, they used teacher-made tests, observed students working in small groups, and even set aside time to talk with the other grade-level teachers to compare and contrast the work of their respective students to get a broader perspective.

All teachers met midyear to report what they had done, how, and the effect it was having. This meeting was also used to reconfirm the commitment to this approach. Teachers report seeing an improvement in student learning, and the principal is pleased that this vision has resulted in a sharper focus on student learning.

Now let's examine how to use the building blocks from chapter 1 (getting buy-in, starting with an early win, and providing ongoing support) to see how they apply to learning instruction.

GETTING BUY-IN: "WE'RE ALL IN THIS TOGETHER"

It's wonderful when teachers see or are brought to see the benefits of the instructional vision. The effective leader can bring these teachers to a new level of greatness as a result. Getting buy-in from the willing is not an issue. These are likely the people who helped the leader develop the vision in the first place. The issue is how to get buy-in from those who don't see what's in it for them or who are comfortable and satisfied with things are now.

Likely there are teachers who support the change and some who are opposed—but the majority will be in the middle. These are folks whose buy-in is especially important. Fortunately, there are techniques to assist this. An important use of data, as described in the previous section, is to raise awareness of what is working well and what needs improvement. Objective measures are important for getting buy-in so everyone can see the evidence. An elementary school principal in Florida uses teacher surveys to get input on strengths and weaknesses of the school's instructional program.

First, the leader needs to find out if teacher resistance comes from a lack of skill or that teachers are not convinced that the vision will result in a positive change. The former is relatively easy to address through professional development, coaching, and feedback.

More problematic is when teachers don't see the value in the vision or see the value but don't consider it important enough to be worth the effort. The leader is in the position of having to demonstrate the value in the short term so there is confidence that putting in the effort will be worth it in the long term. This can be accomplished by having teacher leaders play a key role with their colleagues. Peer-learning activities and demonstrations by trusted colleagues also help.

This works well and not only at the school level but also at the district level.

One innovative superintendent strongly believes in the power of peer collaboration to improve instruction within the school community and between schools. She has created districtwide programs of peer learning in which host schools and two additional schools share and learn together. In fact, so much importance is placed on these learning partner arrangements that the district and the administrators' union have made the master principal position an official position covered by union contract, with an additional stipend for exemplary principals who agree to coach and mentor new or aspiring principals or serve as hosts for the learning partners schools.

It needs to be remembered that, when trying to get buy-in, just as in building a culture on values, it isn't necessary that the participants fully appreciate the vision for the same reason that the leadership team is putting it forth. It matters that the leaders appeal to the self-interest and perceptions of the faculty members. How will this vision help them achieve more of their own goals for students?

Of course, one of the best ways to get buy-in is to start with that early win.

STARTING WITH AN EARLY WIN

Let's start this section by describing what an early win in instruction is *not*. Improving test scores in reading and mathematics by the end of the year is *not* an early win! Banking on such an improvement as the demonstration of instruction improvements is a poor bet. First of all, everyone has to wait until June to see the results — and, once the results are in, that's that. There is no chance to make further improvements. It's an all-in strategy that is way too risky.

An early win entails starting with the end in mind (those June test scores) and thinking through the steps along the way so everyone will be able to see progress toward the goal. What can be done in September that will demonstrate (with evidence) that we are on the right track?

> Here's an example of how one large district used an early win to ultimately bring about a districtwide program that helped teachers and students. The early win was a pilot, in four schools, of short-term assessments that provided ongoing feedback to teachers every six weeks about their students' progress. It was an attempt to see if learning would be accelerated. And, indeed, that was the case. Even a thirteen-year teacher reported that "I see the difference in my teaching." Peer visits confirmed this.
>
> The ongoing data and discussions about how to use them to improve learning for children helped everyone see the vision, which was not about effective instruction but rather whether students were learning. The results were also data-rich, with documented improvements in student learning in the four pilot schools. Needless to say, the next year, there were fifty-six additional schools that wanted to use this program. That's an example of how an early win can be used to demonstrate results and build momentum.

And, remember the school previously in this chapter that was implementing the parent-involvement model? Even though it is going well now, this wasn't always the case. Although the teachers valued the new partnerships, the new approach involved much new preparation, skill, and effort. An early win turned the tide. Once a small group of teachers tried the model and were successful, their success was celebrated at a schoolwide event. It was apparent that the benefits outweighed the costs and that this was doable. Building on this momentum, the program then was able to be implemented schoolwide.

PROVIDING ONGOING SUPPORT

Perhaps the most important source of ongoing support—provided by the district or the school or both—is professional development. This takes several forms, such as workshops, engaging faculty meetings, job-embedded professional development, protocols and tools, teachers visiting other teachers and discussing their lessons afterward, and support from the principal's supervisor, the principal, and the assistant principal.

However, time and again, when principals are asked what the single most important ongoing support they can offer that has led to success, the answer is instructional coaches. Such coaches are the very definition of ongoing support because they are available on a daily basis to model lessons, observe classroom activities, provide advice, share the latest thinking on the content of their specialty content area, ask critical questions to improve teacher practice, and be a sounding board and thought partner to help solve problems. Every day. Finding resources to pay for coaches is one of the most important structural aspects leaders can do to improve instruction.

See It in Action: Principal-Led Instructional Improvements 🎞

Two detailed examples of principals who have developed innovative approaches to improving instruction have been developed by Public Broadcasting Service affiliate WNET. They may be found at http://bit.ly/highpayoff4.

The principals in this video have built instructional leadership capacity among the teaching and administrative staff. We see instructional council meetings, the work of teacher leaders, and visitations among teachers.

There is much observable collaboration and teachers opening their classrooms and wanting to assist their colleagues. And we see the principals scheduling the time teachers need for professional development, including meetings held across subject areas and among grade levels,

The schools demonstrate how professional development is delivered. The use of "grade level chairs" is explored in enhancing professional development. There is a theme of building capacity. In this regard, use of teacher leaders is illustrated. The teacher leaders become staff developers. One school shows how they developed a "go to" list where each teacher's strengths are publicized so others can call upon them for this expertise.

WHAT CAN GET IN THE WAY?

With all the best of intensions, instructional leadership can go astray. Here are some pitfalls to avoid.

- Observing without coaching

  An all-too-common observation among those in NSIP is that when leaders analyze their time use, they find that they are spending time in walkthroughs and observations. That's good, right? Not really—because they are not following up with feedback and coaching. Observing a lesson without feedback not only misses an opportunity to discuss strengths and areas for improvement with the faculty member but also it sends exactly the opposite message—that the purpose of the observation is compliance and monitoring. Neither of these activities is particularly effective in improving instruction.

- Being reactive instead of proactive

  If the leader's mind-set is compliance—with teacher evaluation requirements, student test score requirements, and so on—then it isn't leadership. Effective leaders, such as those who were interviewed for this book, have a vision and focus and make the mandates work *for* them. If the leader knows what should happen to improve instruction, ways will be found to use requirements in the service of those goals.

Teacher evaluation is a good example. There may be requirements for this activity, but there is no requirement *against u*sing this activity as an opportunity for coaching and ongoing support!

- Trying to be a jack-of-all-trades

  If the goal is to turn all activities into those that further instruction, it is clear that the leader cannot do this alone. Principals and district leaders clearly cannot expect to have expertise in every subject area — especially at the middle and high school levels. The answer here is to develop assistant principals and teacher leaders who can engage in these content-specific activities frequently with faculty members. The principal's and district leader's job is to develop and facilitate the networking of these leaders.

- Avoiding the most challenged staff

  It is human nature to try to avoid uncomfortable situations. Unfortunately that isn't possible when trying to improve instruction in districts and schools. One of the most important — and most difficult — jobs of the leader is trying to improve the performance of those who are having the most difficulty performing well. It is much more fun to spend time in the classrooms of teachers who are inspiring and engaging with their students. But, it is of paramount importance that school leaders spend time with teachers who are having difficulty and district leaders spend time with principals who are having a hard time. These are the people who need the most support if instruction is going to improve schoolwide or districtwide.

Therefore, there is much a leader can do to improve instruction even though not working directly with students. Fortunately there is a tool to assist the leader in assessing the attitudes and aptitudes of those who do provide direct instruction that will provide the vision, data, buy-in, and help to plan the early win and identify ways of providing ongoing support. That tool is presented in chapter 6.

Chapter **6**

Using Data to Plan Instructional Improvement Strategies

There are many ways in which data inform the furthering of the vision for instructional improvement. Data may be used (1) to assess student needs and progress; (2) as the basis for planning activities that support the achievement of the strategy's vision; (3) to set benchmarks to measure progress and make midcourse corrections; and (4) to set outcome indicators so everyone will know when the vision has been achieved. Data are also used to frame all discussions in high-performing schools. What are the trends across disciplines? Across grade levels? For the school? For the district? What type of immediate feedback is relevant?

A Georgia principal says that the first thing she did when arriving at her school was bring individual groups together by grade level so teachers could really look at the data. They defined long-term and short-term goals. "We sit with each teacher twice a year and talk about the data," she says. "The data is information but it is the conversation that allows me to talk about our responsibilities for our children." Another principal concurs: "We are data-driven.... Teachers develop goals based on data and create plans to address the weaknesses." She and her teachers use student data to understand each child based on as many data points as possible.

In addition, the use of data is important for planning and developing benchmarks and to measure success. In a Kentucky high school, the principal, assistant principals, teachers, and math coach meet with individual students and groups of students to set goals for state tests based on data.

A high school uses graduation data coaches who meet twice a week to keep track of all students in the graduating class and monitor their attendance, achievement, and grades. This ensures that they are all on track for graduation and — if not — that appropriate interventions are taken.

At the district level, the superintendent and principal supervisors assist school leaders by providing timely, accurate data via a districtwide student information system. This system provides schoolwide data as well as data for each teacher's reflection and ability to make quick changes. The system also provides online resources for teachers and leaders to explore when they are investigating new approaches for specific student's issues. This includes research and university reports as well as blogs from other teachers and leaders about how they have successfully addressed specific instructional issues.

ASSESSING READINESS WITH THE AAA TOOL

The Assessing Attitudes and Aptitudes Tool (AAA) is an instrument that has been used to assess educator attitudes, self-perceived skills, and behaviors regarding the main aspects of interactive pedagogy that encourages students' critical thinking in schools and districts in the United States and internationally, in other words, their *readiness* to engage in new instructional practices. This instrument is used to perform beginning needs assessments and readiness assessments — resulting in strategic plans for teacher training and professional development. It can also be used as a pretest and a posttest to evaluate the effectiveness of teacher-training programs — comparing readiness levels at the beginning with those after the program.

The instrument consists of statements regarding principles and practices of effective instruction in these topic areas:

- Education concepts and philosophies
- Principles of student learning
- Curriculum development
- Instructional methods
- Assessment of student progress

There are forty-one statements in which respondents are asked to respond to two questions: (1) how important is this? (measuring attitude) and (2) how is it reflected in your practice? (or your self-rating) (measuring skills). There are two responses required for each statement in sections A–E: one that is a measure of attitude and the other of self-perceived skill. The instrument has content validity and, as such, reflects the vision of numerous educators. You can use either the entire instrument or select the items that are most relevant to the instructional improvements you are trying to lead.

The surveys are administered anonymously. The resulting data can therefore inform four aspects of your strategy:

1. How ready the respondents are to participate in instructional improvement in each instructional topic area (the total mean score for all questions in each section). If the readiness is high, you're good to go.

2. If the readiness is not as high as you'd like, where does it need bolstering?

    a. Attitudes (mean score of the perceived importance items).

    b. Skills (mean score of the perceived self-ratings or degree reflected in practice).

       There are different activities needed to raise readiness depending if what's needed is better appreciation for importance (the need to demonstrate how and why the specific activity leads to better instruction) or skills (the importance is appreciated but participants don't know how to pull it off, so skills training would be in order).

3. For which items do attitudes need improvement? For which are skills development needed? (item analyses)

4. When a second administration is done at a benchmark time, have attitudes and skills improved? (pre-post analysis)

Here's a summary of the AAA data and to what uses it can be put.

Data Analysis	What It Measures	What It Shows	How It Can Be Used
Mean scores for importance	Attitudes for activities in each instructional area	Whether, in general, there is strong support for the general area	If attitudes are good, capitalize on this; if they aren't, develop activities that will convince people of their value.
Mean scores for self-rating or degree reflected in practice	Skill assessment for activities in each instructional area	Whether, in general, respondents believe they have the skills needed	If they do, then nothing is needed; if skills need improvement, professional development and coaching should be planned.
Mean score for each item analysis	Attitude and skill assessment for each individual set of statements	For which specific items are there the best or worst attitudes and skills	Make a plan for specific evidence demonstrations (for attitude improvement) and specific content of coaching or professional development.
Pre-post analysis	All scores from the first administration to the next	Whether there has been progress in improving attitudes and skills	Celebrate successes; make plans for further improvement.

THE ASSESSING ATTITUDES AND APTITUDES (AAA) TOOL

Note: A Google Docs version of this tool is online at. https://drive.google .com/templates?view=public&authorId=09213941696829242278

To access the tool from this URL, click on "Use this template." Click on "File" and "Make a copy" to create a copy of the tool for you to send to those you are asking to respond. Next, click on "File" and "Send form." A pop-up box will appear which will allow you to send the form via e-mail and also provides you with a link to the survey that you can embed in your own cover e-mail.

Once respondents have completed the survey, you will find a summary of their responses by clicking on "Reponses" and then "Summary of responses."

The following statements reflect various philosophies of education. By blackening the appropriate circle on the answer sheet that corresponds to the number of the question, please indicate (1) how *important* you believe the concept to be and (2) your assessment of the degree to which your current practice *reflects* this concept.

Here is the paper and pencil version of the tool.

Instructions for Respondents.

Degree to which this is reflected in your practice or self-rating

a. How important is this concept?	4	3	2	1
	Highest importance	Important	A little	Not important
b. Degree to which this is reflected in your practice or self-rating	4	3	2	1
	Highest importance	Important	A little	Not important

A. Education Concepts and Philosophies

1. **Teachers should be the primary constructors of knowledge for students:**
   a. How important is this concept?   4 3 2 1
   b. Degree to which concept is reflected in your practice   4 3 2 1

2. **Students should be the primary constructors of their own knowledge:**
   a. How important is this concept?   4 3 2 1
   b. Degree to which concept is reflected in your practice   4 3 2 1

3. **Teachers should use a variety of pedagogic methods on an ongoing basis as opposed to reliance on any one method:**
   a. How important is this concept?   4 3 2 1
   b. Degree to which concept is reflected in your practice   4 3 2 1

4. **An interactive environment in the classroom is important to facilitate learning:**
   a. How important is this concept?   4 3 2 1
   b. Degree to which concept is reflected in your practice   4 3 2 1

5. **All students are capable of high achievements:**
   a. How important is this concept?   4 3 2 1
   b. Degree to which concept is reflected in your practice   4 3 2 1

6. **All teachers should be teachers of reading:**
   a. How important is this concept?   4 3 2 1
   b. Degree to which concept is reflected in your practice   4 3 2 1

7. **All teachers should be teachers of writing:**
   a. How important is this concept?   4 3 2 1
   b. Degree to which concept is reflected in your practice   4 3 2 1

8. **Teachers should read the current educational publications to keep current with the state of the field:**
   a. How important is this concept?   4 3 2 1
   b. Degree to which concept is reflected in your practice   4 3 2 1

9. **Teachers should belong to and be active in professional associations:**
   a. How important is this concept?   4 4 2 1
   b. Degree to which concept is reflected in your practice   4 3 2 1

B. Principles of Student Learning

10. **Ability to analyze the readiness level of your classes:**
    a. How important is this concept?   4 3 2 1
    b. Self-rating   4 3 2 1

11. **Ability to match instructional strategies to the readiness of your classes:**
    a. How important is this concept?   4 3 2 1
    b. Self-rating   4 3 2 1

12. **Diagnosing the learning needs of the students in your classes:**
    a. How important is this concept?   4 3 2 1
    b. Self-rating   4 3 2 1

13. **Incorporating student needs into the classes:**
    a. How important is this concept?   4 3 2 1
    b. Self-rating   4 3 2 1

14. **Establishing a classroom environment that encourages and supports critical thinking:**
    a. How important is this concept?   4 3 2 1
    b. Self-rating   4 3 2 1

C. Curriculum and Materials Development

15. **Developing appropriate instructional objectives:**
    a. How important is this concept?   4 3 2 1
    b. Self-rating   4 3 2 1

16. **Identifying appropriate curriculum and instructional materials:**
    a. How important is this concept?   4 4 2 1
    b. Self-rating   4 3 2 1

17. **Infusing reading throughout the curriculum:**
    a. How important is this concept?   4 3 2 1
    b. Self-rating   4 3 2 1

18. **Infusing writing throughout the curriculum:**
    a. How important is this concept?   4 3 2 1
    b. Self-rating   4 3 2 1

(continued)

19. **Choosing appropriate textbooks or writing new materials:**
    a. How important is this concept?　　　　4　3　2　1
    b. Self-rating　　　　4　3　2　1

20. **Writing new lessons and instructional materials:**
    a. How important is this concept?　　　　4　3　2　1
    b. Self-rating　　　　4　3　2　1

21. **Adapting existing lessons and instructional materials:**
    a. How important is this concept?　　　　4　3　2　1
    b. Self-rating　　　　4　3　2　1

D. Instruction Delivery Methods

22. **Using interdisciplinary instruction:**
    a. How important is this concept?　　　　4　3　2　1
    b. Self-rating　　　　4　3　2　1

23. **Using instructional activities that facilitate critical thinking for your students:**
    a. How important is this concept?　　　　4　3　2　1
    b. Self-rating　　　　4　3　2　1

24. **Using effective questioning techniques:**
    a. How important is this concept?　　　　4　3　2　1
    b. Self-rating　　　　4　3　2　1

25. **Providing opportunities for your students to apply what they have learned:**
    a. How important is this concept?　　　　4　3　2　1
    b. Self-rating　　　　4　3　2　1

26. **Encouraging students' active participation:**
    a. How important is this concept?　　　　4　3　2　1
    b. Self-rating　　　　4　3　2　1

27. **Using instructional activities that involve your students in problem solving:**
    a. How important is this concept?　　　　4　3　2　1
    b. Self-rating　　　　4　3　2　1

28. **Using simulations in your teaching:**
    a. How important is this concept? 4 3 2 1
    b. Self-rating 4 3 2 1

29. **Using group and cooperative learning in your teaching:**
    a. How important is this concept? 4 3 2 1
    b. Self-rating 4 3 2 1

30. **Teaching all children to respect differences between them:**
    a. How important is this concept? 4 3 2 1
    b. Self-rating 4 3 2 1

31. **Differentiating students' tasks by how they individually learn best:**
    a. How important is this concept? 4 3 2 1
    b. Self-rating 4 3 2 1

32. **Having students share their own writing:**
    a. How important is this concept? 4 3 2 1
    b. Self-rating 4 3 2 1

33. **Having students critique the writing of their peers:**
    a. How important is this concept? 4 3 2 1
    b. Self-rating 4 3 2 1

34. **Providing modeled writing for student:**
    a. How important is this concept? 4 3 2 1
    b. Self-rating 4 3 2 1

35. **Discussing with students why the modeled writing is exemplary:**
    a. How important is this concept? 4 3 2 1
    b. Self-rating 4 3 2 1

E. Evaluation and Assessment

36. **Determining appropriate performance standards for your classes:**
    a. How important is this concept?   4 3 2 1
    b. Self-rating   4 3 2 1

37. **Ensuring that all students are aware of and understand the standards:**
    a. How important is this concept?   4 3 2 1
    b. Self-rating   4 3 2 1

38. **Monitoring and evaluating the progress of your students:**
    a. How important is this concept?   4 3 2 1
    b. Self-rating   4 3 2 1

39. **Developing appropriate instruments to test students' comprehension and ability to apply the subject:**
    a. How important is this concept?   4 3 2 1
    b. Self-rating   4 3 2 1

40. **Providing frequent benchmarks during the semester to evaluate student progress:**
    a. How important is this concept?   4 3 2 1
    b. Self-rating   4 3 2 1

41. **Providing regular feedback to students on their classroom achievement:**
    a. How important is this concept?   4 3 2 1
    b. Self-rating   4 3 2 1

USEFUL ANALYSES

There are many analyses that can be done with the data to tell the leader about the readiness of the respondents for instructional improvements and what activities that might be considered as a result. Here are a couple:

Item Analyses

Attitudes (high scores are between 4 and 3; low scores are between 1 and 2)

- Which are the sections or items with the highest attitude ratings? What are those average scores? Building on these is a good idea.

- Which are the sections or items with the lowest attitude ratings? How low are they (what are the scores)? Might these attitudes disrupt the instruction strategy? If so, how will you seek to improve them?

Skills (high scores are between 4 and 3; low scores are between 1 and 2)

- Which are the sections or items with the highest skills ratings? What are those average scores? Building on these is a good idea.

- Which are the sections or items with the lowest skills ratings? How low are they (what are the scores)? Might these skills disrupt the instruction strategy? If so, how will you seek to improve them?

Readiness assessment: Attitudes plus skills overall (for each section)

- Quadrant I: Low scores for both attitudes and skills. These are means of 1.4 and below for both skill and attitude. Or 100% rating 1 or 2 for both attitude and skills if you are using the URL.

- The implication here is that you will need to do both skill building and attitude improvement. Again, early wins — and peer pressure — will be needed.

- Quadrant II: High scores for attitudes, but low scores for skills. These are average scores of 3.5 and above for attitude and below 1.5 for skill. Or 100% rating 4 or 3 for attitude with 100% rating 1 or 2 for skills if you are using the URL version.

AAA Mean Score Analysis for Paper and Pencil Version

High attitude

QUADRANT II: High attitude/Low skills (3.5 or above for attitude/ 1.5 or below for skills) Our mean scores are: ___ for attitudes ___ for skills	**QUADRANT III:** High attitude/High skills (3.5 or above for both attitude and skills) Our mean scores are: ___ for attitudes ___ for skills
QUADRANT I: Low attitude/Low skills (1.4 and below for both attitude and skills) Our mean scores are: ___ for attitudes ___ for skills	**QUADRANT IV:** Low attitude/High skills (1.5 and below for attitude/ 3.5 and above for skills) Our mean scores are: ___ for attitudes ___ for skills

Attitude (vertical axis) — Low attitude

Low skills — **Skills** — High skills

AAA Percent Analysis for Googleforms Version

High attitude

QUADRANT II: High attitude/Low skills (100% 3 or 4 for attitude/ 100% 1 or 2 for skills) Our score is: ___% with 3 or 5 for attitudes and ___% with 1 or 2 for skills	**QUADRANT III:** High attitude/High skills (100% rating 3 or 4 in both) Our score is: ___% with 3 or 4 for attitudes and ___% with 3 or 4 for skills
QUADRANT I: Low attitude/Low skills (100% rating 1 or 2 in both) Our score is: ___% with 1 or 2 for attitudes and ___% with 1 or 2 for skills	**QUADRANT IV:** Low attitude/High skills (100% 1 or 2 for attitude/ 100% 3 or 4 for skills) Our score is: ___% with 1 or 2 for attitudes and ___% with 3 or 4 for skills

Attitude (vertical axis) — Low attitude

Low skills — **Skills** — High skills

- The implication here is that, with some professional development, these folks should be good contributors.

- Quadrant III: High scores for both skills and attitudes? These are average scores of 3.5 and above for both attitudes and skills. Or 100% having scores of 3 or 4 for both (if you're using the URL at the front of this chapter).

The implication here is that, with these folks, you're ready to go.

- Quadrant IV: Low scores for attitudes, but high scores for skills. These are average scores of 3.5 and above for skills and below 1.5 for attitude. Or 100% rating 1 or 2 for attitude with 100% rating 3 or 4 for skills.

The implication here is that you will need to convince these participants of the value of the endeavor, and when that happens, they will be up to the task. Early wins work well here.

One final note: Please be aware that you might be surprised at what you learn from using this tool. Many principals have reported that assessing readiness has been the single most important activity they have done when planning strategies to improve instruction. Several principals have often found that ideas that seemed exciting and worthwhile were spurned by faculty as adding too much extra work—and that other activities would have to be foregone.

On the other hand, a principal who thought the teachers would not want one more activity on their plate was pleasantly surprised to find out that they were ready and willing to include a new reading program in the year's curriculum. Another principal learned that there was big support at his elementary school for piloting a "departmental" approach, rather than having one teacher stay with the same class all day. Testing these assumptions is always a good idea.

Part 3

Strategy: Learning Communities

Chapter 7

Facilitating Learning Communities

Math scores are now the highest in the school's history. That's due to the learning community.

— An elementary school principal

Developing and facilitating learning communities is a high-payoff strategy whereby group members engage together in solving common problems directly correlated with improving student achievement and building on the culture. Research has found that such learning communities are "a strong predictor of instructional practices that are strongly associated with student achievement" (Louis, 2009, p. 37).

This strategy goes by many different names. Sometimes called *professional learning communities, communities of practice, peer learning, data teams, inquiry groups, learning teams,* or other labels, they nevertheless have several characteristics in common. The learning community is ongoing and results oriented. The community defines and contributes model practices, tools, curriculum, or other agreed-on products for use by the community and for others in the school or district. There is a clear vision of an instruction-centered goal. This is active and mutual learning, not learning just for the sake of learning.

It is a real-time strategy in which participants define a problem of practice and devise ways to address it based on what each participant brings to the table. The aim is for everyone to make good use of what is developed to strengthen his or her own ongoing practices. It is continual, job-embedded learning—that refresher we spoke about in chapter 1.

This goes well beyond individual learning and having good, collegial conversations. The learning community should result in products that inform the community members and can also be shared with the full district or school to assist others as well. This happens via regular meetings as well as other activities in-between meetings such as assignments that participants bring back to the group.

The learning community is not an add-on to everyone's work. It *is* the work. Learning communities are supportive and further the work that everyone is engaged with and helps everyone do his or her job better. For learning communities to work at their best, the culture should support those instruction-centered values described in chapter 4, particularly learning, teamwork, risk taking, trust, and learning from mistakes. If any of these values are not present, the successful learning community strategy helps to build them.

So, by whatever name it is known, let's call them *learning communities* here and define them as ongoing, coordinated activities geared to learning together to further instructional objectives in the context of the culture.

PURPOSE AND GOALS

Because learning communities support the achievement of leading instruction strategy, it is important that the leadership team consider the guidance in chapters 5 and 6 first. Then learning communities know what outcomes they want to address and can decide on their topic, problem(s) of practice, and early wins. Typically they deal with such topics as literacy across the curriculum, writing across the curriculum, improving instruction in the content areas, and using data to define and address common problems of instructional practice.

LEARNING METHODS

Learning communities use engaging and collegial learning methods such as analysis of data, reading books and discussing their implications, teacher demonstration lessons and discussions, focus groups with students, common review of student work, visitation with teachers in other schools, and exploring the latest research, among other methods. Bringing in outside experts from time to time — or sending some learning community members to conferences — is useful because it provides outside perspectives and motivation.

There are strict rules of engagement that center on the commitment of all group members to each other and to the work: meetings must not be canceled (they are top priority), all members attend all meetings, and data (as opposed to unsubstantiated opinion) rules! Often the learning communities ask participants to sign compacts or contracts in which these commitments are made explicit.

STRUCTURES

The communities are organized into different groups at different times. It is important that each learning community has the participants needed for the job. It is also important that people experience being in different groups at different times for different perspectives. For example, some learning communities might be organized by discipline, others by grade level, others by "critical friends" members, still others might be a mix of feeder pattern grades (third grade with fourth grade, for example), or a mix of participants from across the school or district.

Some learning communities might have rotating chairs. The principal or district leaders are not always or often the community leaders. They must be sincere in wanting to learn alongside everyone else. The learning communities are an excellent opportunity for listening. Often the leader, however, will provide common templates (see the "Learning Together Templates" in chapter 8) so there is a common structure to all the learning communities and they can come up with the same type of product or result.

The leader makes it convenient for the groups to meet, usually a common meeting time each week. Principals interviewed revealed that some had half-day meetings every Wednesday and others scheduled forty minutes on Monday or Wednesday afternoons. What matters is the consistency of the scheduling—and that all learning community members have the same schedule. Of course, as we saw in chapter 4, leaders need to make sure that the planned learning community time does not conflict with members' other values, such as needing to leave to pick up their children from other settings.

DISTRICT-LEVEL LEARNING COMMUNITIES

Districts can help make this happen for all schools, and the principal can make this happen within the school. District leaders conduct learning communities for school leaders across the district. They may also support school learning communities by facilitating them and serving as outside experts. They may also facilitate visits to other schools within the district.

One leader used a learning community to help the district plan its instructional priorities. She identified a core group of principals and other leaders throughout the district and embarked on a book study of new curriculum and instructional methods. As this group studied together, they determined that they needed a strategy for helping others in the district understand the new content and methods. They are currently working on setting up learning communities in all schools that will do similar book studies and advise the district going forward.

Here's an example of an effective learning community in a suburban district high school. A low-performing high school was transformed into a high-performing school, and the principal credits the learning community strategy. Many students were not doing well in reading and math, so the leadership team developed learning communities in each of these two areas. The charge to these ongoing groups was to use data to identify struggling students and figure out why they weren't learning the core reading and math skills. This contrasted with the former attitude of "just keep going."

The groups met regularly throughout the semester (during time scheduled by the principal). They rotated the chair, analyzed the data, brought different perspectives to discuss, reviewed student work, discussed the problem with students, and came up with an important conclusion and a proposal.

The learning community reported back to the full faculty at the end of the semester and there was a complete discussion. The finding was that students needed more assistance with reading and math than teachers could provide in the context of their courses. The recommendation was that a reading and math support center be created where any student could come to receive additional one-on-one tutoring and support.

The leadership team, knowing a good idea when they heard one, embraced this learning community–developed solution and authorized the creation of this center. Space was provided; teachers were hired for extended, paid hours; and a full-time teacher was hired to staff the center.

Not only was the learning community successful but also their idea had been put into action—and student achievement was apparent the very next semester. It was important that something practical emerged from the learning community's analysis and discussions—and that the leadership team was responsive and able to shift resources to its creation. The learning community now has great credibility (and an important symbol of its success in the center). It still meets regularly because they never run out of problems of practice to address!

ADVICE FOR PLANNERS AND FACILITATORS

Planning these sessions and the work in-between sessions is different from developing a workshop or course. A course is designed to deliver understanding and use of specific content. Even though the most effective workshops are reality-based and interactive—they are still content-based. Learning communities are different—they are based in problem solving with no prescribed content other than that which participants bring in as appropriate.

Therefore, planning effective learning communities is more dependent on group problem identification and design of a product or resource to help them and others address the problem. The learning is problem-based, not content-based. The learning community needs to go where it needs to go as the needs develop in real time. Adaptability and flexibility are important.

Facilitating such a group entails getting the best out of each participant: thinking on one's feet about what is being said and how each contribution can combine with others to make progress. And, facilitation is firmly about enforcing the ground rules, without which the group is likely to dissolve into chaos:

1. The facilitator presents a problem statement.
2. Participants speak to the specifics of the topic being discussed.
3. Contributions should be based on data and evidence, not opinion.
4. No personal statements about anyone are permitted.
5. Everyone listens respectfully to each other.
6. Ultimately, the question is whether each member can support the group's decision (not whether everyone agrees it is the best approach).

Planners often underestimate the importance of ground rules. Especially for low-readiness groups, ground rules are a must. If people are inexperienced working in learning communities or have had unsuccessful experience, they will not know what to do. They will truly appreciate the structure and guidance. This became apparent to an assistant principal who was trying to conduct a learning community. She reported that the group was meeting, but not moving. What finally unstuck the group was spending a full meeting agreeing on the ground rules. From then on, the work proceeded well and resulted in needed changes to the science curriculum, the group's goal. A year later, the group was still meeting productively.

In the following sections, we'll explore using the building blocks of strategy to lead improvements in instruction, that is, getting buy-in, starting with an early win, and providing ongoing support.

GETTING BUY-IN: "WE'RE ALL IN THIS TOGETHER"

The leader has goals for students based on the instructional vision of the school. It is, however, important that teachers also are satisfied and fulfilled. One way to build in this "what's in it for me" is through promoting learning and growth for the adults in the community. Many are familiar with philosopher Abraham Maslow's hierarchy of needs, a motivational framework that demonstrates that most people have a need to learn, grow, and self-actualize. Therefore, most people are motivated by learning on the job and achieving satisfaction. The learning community is a natural outlet for this to happen. Everyone has an ongoing learning experience that also helps improve their teaching practice. One principal cited as a great moment in the life of the learning community when teachers were able to say "I'm struggling with this."

In order for this learning and growth to be motivational, however, it has to correspond to the *perceived* needs of each individual. Each person needs to define his or her own learning needs. These may or may not be the same as what the leader wants the person to learn. A balance point must be reached. Nonetheless, the learning communities need to be based on a combination of what all agree to be the most important learning to achieve the instruction-improvement strategy.

The leader needs to identify those self-perceived learning needs, analyze the similarities and differences between those and what needs to be learned to achieve the instruction strategy result, and plan the learning communities accordingly. The "Participants' Needs Assessment Template" in chapter 8 should help with this.

STARTING WITH AN EARLY WIN

The first work product of the learning community is a good example of an early win—not only for the learning community strategy but also for the instructional strategy. It is, therefore, particularly important that the learning community selects an effective early win to pursue. Several principals have remarked that there was some resentment or opposition to the learning community when it was initially proposed, but "once the math achievement/reading achievement went up, the resentment want away."

Remember that these are not June scores on standardized tests—the early win can be measured by teacher evaluation of student work, portfolio assessment, student presentations, or scores on teacher-made quizzes. The idea is to implement the activity, tool, or teaching practice developed by the learning community and observe the difference it makes for students in the near term.

Because this is an early look, it is possible to invent new activities if it turns out that the first try by the learning community did not result in improved student learning. If that is the case, the next job of the learning community is to ask why and develop new activities to try to address what's missing.

In one urban middle school seeking to improve ELA instruction, the learning community decided to start out by reading a book together to get a common understanding of the issues. The session where they discussed that book was an early win. It demonstrated to participants the usefulness of such a group discussion and also confirmed everyone's commitment to undertaking assignments. After this session, commitment to the learning community was high. Attendance was mandatory and the weekly sessions could not be canceled. The learning community was top priority!

PROVIDING ONGOING SUPPORT

A learning community needs several ongoing supports, for example, a regular time to meet and access to timely and accurate data. However, there is one ongoing support that is indispensable—someone who is assigned to be the facilitator (sometimes called a *coach*).

This is the person who is responsible for monitoring the work plan and making sure that the work is moving along apace and that deadlines are met. The facilitator often does more than give people friendly reminders—he or she often is someone who makes things happen, such as synthesizing responses or data provided by learning community members for the next meeting.

SEE IT IN ACTION: WORKING WITH LEARNING COMMUNITIES 🎬

An example of how an assistant principal has effectively used a learning community to improve instruction for his students has been developed by Public Broadcasting Service affiliate WNET. It is in the section "Cultivating Leadership in Others," and may be found at http://bit.ly/highpayoff5.

You'll see the assistant principal of administration lead the school's biology learning community and how the principal coaches him along the way. Through the biology learning community, teachers have made enhancements, student performance has improved, and the assistant principal has learned a great deal about learning communities as a vehicle to lead instruction, both for students and for teachers.

WHAT CAN GET IN THE WAY?

A recent survey of principals in North Dakota found that they considered conducting the learning community to be important, but it was their most difficult undertaking. They are right. Here are some reasons why.

Lack of Focus

The single biggest obstacle is that participants often have trouble narrowing the scope of what the group will address. Sometimes these results come from over-enthusiasm for what the group will be able to do; other times it stems from needing to develop a muscle to truly hone in on what is most important and doable. It is the learning community equivalent of "I didn't have time to write you a short letter, so I wrote you a long one."

It is easier to talk in generalities than to drill down to specifics—especially in a group setting. The broader the discussion, the easier it is to get consensus. However, what you get is a group that either talks endlessly about its purpose or—if it sets to work on a broad area—gets bogged down in ideas at the expense of accomplishing anything. The key to avoiding this barrier is to have a good facilitator who leads the group to drill down on specifics. The facilitator's template in chapter 8 should help.

Seen as an Add-On

Because learning communities represent an ongoing time commitment, participants will be resentful if what's in it for them is not readily apparent. This commonly results from the work of the learning community being separate and apart from the work participants do on a daily basis. Without alignment—if people can't take what they are doing in the learning community and integrate it with their classes and their students—they will see it as something they are being asked to do "for the good of the school or district" and be less interested and less willing to put forth the effort.

The best way to avoid this potential obstacle is to be very clear and specific about the result—and have all learning community members buy in to that result. Something else that is often effective is to have as a ground rule that the group will often ask the question, is what we are doing directly applicable to our teaching? If the answer is no, the facilitator scraps the rest of the agenda and the group goes on to another topic that is seen as directly applicable.

Not Having the Option to Fail

Learning community members must be permitted to experiment and fail as long as they monitor their work with data. The culture needs to be respectful of risk taking and learning from mistakes so groups feel free to take risks that might push the envelope to solve difficult problems. Playing it safe won't get many innovative solutions. Learning communities need to be adaptable and flexible because their destination and content can't be known at the beginning. They need to go where they need to go as the work evolves.

Leaders Dominate the Discussion

The goal to learn together must be genuine. Learning communities are not a forum for the leaders to share their wisdom and opinions. Everyone is an equal player in these communities; everyone has an important voice.

Leaders need to respect this and enable participation and collaboration. When possible, leaders should not be the facilitators of the learning community. These communities are a great chance for leaders to listen and contribute — not to lead or dominate.

What follows in chapter 8 are templates that can guide the planning and conducting of successful learning communities for (1) the participants, (2) the planners, and (3) the facilitator, and a template for keeping track of the decisions made.

Using Data to Plan Learning Community Strategies

All learning communities use data to identify and analyze the problem of practice and to provide evidence for use in discussions — and to stay away from unsubstantiated opinions. A specific type of learning community is a *data team* or an *inquiry team,* but use of data is essential for the learning community's work. Data help identify the issues and trends to inform goal setting and product development. It also informs the development of midcourse corrections when used to set milestone check-ins.

Data are also helpful because often people don't know what they don't know. The data will inform individuals of areas in which they might want some skills refreshed or expertise from colleagues.

LEARNING TOGETHER TEMPLATES

The following four templates may prove useful in implementing the guidance offered in chapter 7. They include a template to be completed by different learning community participants:

- Each participant: to ensure buy-in and that each person's learning needs are taken into account in the planning of the learning community

- The planners of the learning community: to ensure that they are taking into account all relevant factors when developing the learning community

- The facilitator of the learning community: to ensure successful implementation for the group during each session and in-between

- Sample learning community recording work plan

These templates help the learning community to walk the talk of mutual learning and problem solving. The first step is to hear all voices in the planning — the defining of the instruction-centered goal by the leadership team — and then the input of the potential participants on what would constitute success and their individual learning goals (participant template).

That serves as the basis for planning the problem or practice, learning methods, group membership, and data and other resources that will best meet the needs of the participants and the instruction-centered goal of the school or district (input for the learning community planner's template). The participant template also serves as reworking of the first learning community meeting—a necessary ingredient to demonstrate the seriousness of the learning community's work and everyone's mutual commitment to the group.

The third template for the facilitator itemizes the steps the conductor of the meeting needs to take to lead a productive session. The fourth template is a meeting plan summary, by which the facilitator ensures that everyone has the same recollection of what was decided and how the group has agreed to move forward.

Participants' Needs Assessment Template

(To Inform the Learning Community Planner)

Here is a template that the planner could distribute to the participants in advance of the meeting in order to accommodate their felt needs into the architecture of the learning community.

We are establishing learning communities to problem-solve and develop new approaches, tools, or products to help us achieve instructional improvements for our students. Your participation will be most valuable. We want to make sure that this effort is worthwhile for everyone and that your personal learning needs are met. Your completion of this survey will help the planners design a learning commmunty to accomplish all these goals.

Please complete by _____ and send or hand in to _____. We look forward to productive sessions.

School or district's instruction-centered goal: *(to be completed by the leadership team)*

_____

_____

_____

_____

Overall goal of the learning community: *(to be completed by the leadership team; include time frame)*

_____

_____

_____

_____

Goal for the first meeting: To discuss various problems of practice we are experiencing and decide, as a group, on the one we focus on at the beginning. Decide on an early win and time lines.

_____

_____

_____

Suggested problem of practice I'd like the group to address. Please describe only one and be specific.		
How would I define success for the learning community? What are the quantitative goals?		
My personal learning goal:		
How I seek to learn it (please X no more than three methods):		
__Data analysis	__Read articles and books	__Model lessons and discuss
__Group discussion	__Bring back student feedback	__Visitation in school
__Outside experts	__Visitation within district	__Attend conference
__Workshops	__Explore the latest research	__Other (specify):
Membership: Whose expertise might be useful to achieve the group's goal? *Note: Within a diverse group, homogenous subgroups may be created with participants who learn similarly, have various perspectives or experiences, or have the same content expertise.*		
Experience and resources I can contribute:		
What support can leadership provide?		
What data are needed?		
Proposed early win (specific, observable, symbolic, accomplished within three weeks):		
Potential concerns (if any):		

Learning Community Planner's Template

School or district's instruction-centered goal: *(to be completed by the leadership team)*

_____

_____

_____

_____

Overall goal of the learning community: *(to be completed by the leadership team; include time frame)*

_____

_____

_____

_____

Goal for the first meeting: To discuss various problems of practice we are experiencing and decide, as a group, on the one we focus on at the beginning. Decide on an early win and time lines.

I. Analysis of Feedback from Potential Participants

Main (synthesized) problems of practice identified by potential group members:
How would participants define success for the learning community? How would the leadership team define success for the learning community? Is there any discrepancy between these two visions for the learning community? What are they? How might they be resolved?
A compilation of participants' learning goals: Is there any discrepancy between what most people want to learn and the goals of the learning community? If so, what are they and how can they be resolved?

(continued)

Learning methods: How do participants learn best? How many responded to the following methods?		
__Data analysis	__Read articles and books	__Model lessons and discuss
__Group discussion	__Bring back student feedback	__Visitation in school
__Outside experts	__Visitation within district	__Attend conference
__Workshops	__Explore the latest research	__Other (specify):

Membership: Whose expertise might be useful to achieve the group's goal? *Note: Within a diverse group, homogenous subgroups may be created with participants who learn similarly, have various perspectives or experiences, or have the same content expertise.*
Experience and resources identified by members:
What support can leadership provide?
What data are needed? What data are available?
Proposed early wins (specific, observable, symbolic, accomplished within three weeks):
Potential concerns (if any): How can these be alleviated?

II. Additional Planning Considerations

When can sessions be regularly scheduled (making sure there is no conflict with another highly held value)?
Is technical support desirable (computers, virtual space, planning programs, etc.)?

What is the most promising group configuration?

If this is a school learning community, what resources (including personnel) are available from the district office?

Who will be the facilitator for each learning community? Is that person prepared to not only facilitate the group but also develop and monitor the work plan?

Facilitator's Template

School or district's instruction-centered goal: *(to be completed by the leadership team)*

Overall goal of the learning community: *(to be completed by the leadership team; include time frame)*

Goal for the first meeting: To discuss various problems of practice we are experiencing and decide, as a group, on the one we focus on at the beginning. Decide on an early win and time lines.

Present group ground rules:

1. Participants speak to the specifics of the topic being discussed.
2. Contributions should be based on data and evidence, not opinion.
3. No personal statements about anyone are permitted.
4. Everyone listens respectfully to each other.
5. Ultimately, the question is whether each member can support the group's decision (not whether everyone agrees it is the best approach).

(continued)

Define success for the learning community:
Review three prepared problems of practice suggested by the analysis of the participant template. Have the group decide on one.
Methods the group will use (at least to start):
Experience and resources of group members. Ask each member to say what he or she can contribute.
Present support leadership can provide plus any constraints that need to be taken into consideration (such as there is only so much—if any—funding that can be put to the group's work):
What data are needed? What are available?
Proposed early win for the learning community (specific, observable, symbolic, accomplished within three weeks):
Drafting of work plan and plans for assignments and follow-up:

Sample Learning Community Recording or Work Plan

School or district's instruction-centered goal: *(to be completed by the leadership team)*

_____

_____

_____

_____

Overall goal of the learning community: *(to be completed by the leadership team; include time frame)*

_____

_____

_____

_____

Meeting date: _____

Meeting participants: _____

_____

_____

Problem of practice: _____

_____

_____

_____

_____

Early win: _____

_____

_____

_____

WHO is assigned to do...	WHAT...	by WHEN

Part 4

The Payoff

Chapter 9

Using All Strategies Together to Achieve the Vision

> We went from negativity and isolation to collaboration and a focus on instruction.
>
> — A high school principal

Of course, in reality there is a fine line between and among the three high-payoff strategies when it comes to achieving the leader's vision. Although leaders are well served by focusing on one strategy at a time, they all work together and are mutually reinforcing.

In order to achieve the vision, there needs to be a culture with shared values that support the goals the leader seeks. The instruction work needs to be clearly defined and aligned with the vision. And, one of the most effective methods of achieving the instructional efforts is through ongoing learning communities. This chapter tells the stories of education leaders who have combined all three high-payoff strategies and closes with advice on how the tools in this book can be used to align them.

First, let's discuss a superintendent in the Midwest who has brought a laser focus on instruction to her urban district. Through the use of all three high-payoff strategies, this district has been the highest performing in the state for the past several years.

The superintendent has made the value of student success through great teaching and learning the singular focus throughout the district. This shared value formed the basis of the district's "culture of no excuses."

And she walks the talk by providing support—time, funding, and professional development—to all schools. The instructional practices are refined through model schools, which try out innovative curriculum and share their results with schools throughout the district. This was the early win that built momentum.

Ongoing support includes professional development programs for the district's leaders and teachers and ongoing coaching for principals provided by the principal supervisors. Learning communities are a main strategy for ongoing learning. Every Monday for ninety minutes all schools engage in this activity.

Then, there's the middle school where a new English language arts (ELA) curriculum was designed and implemented that illustrates this point. The school's vision was to empower all students to reach for the highest levels to meet the challenges of the twenty-first century and be lifelong learners. The principal and leadership team determined that teaching and learning in ELA needed more rigor in order to fulfill the vision. New curriculum and teaching methods were called for. The instructional strategy would be based on co-teaching and blended learning that would enrich reading on a daily basis.

Because academic rigor and innovative teaching methods were shared values at the school, this strategy seemed consonant with the culture. However, there were many outstanding questions. What type of instruction would be best? How could it be developed and implemented? Where would the time come from to plan this new approach? Would there be sufficient support? Would all this be in addition to teachers' already overburdened workload?

The challenge was turned over to the school's learning community for ELA, which consisted of ELA teachers for all grade levels. The learning community was asked to study the latest methods of instruction in ELA and make recommendations to the leadership team. Learning community members met regularly. They also visited other schools, observing lessons and talking with teachers.

The learning community recommended curriculum and professional development for teachers in co-teaching. The community also recommended that a new type of block scheduling be designed and implemented. This new schedule would provide double-session classes for the co-teachers to have the instructional time they would need with students and also have regularly scheduled planning time.

The principal and leadership team supported all the recommendations. The district chipped in as well, providing an expert in school scheduling.

The principal arranged for ongoing professional development for all teachers. In addition, three teacher leaders were permanently assigned to support this work by offering coaching and demonstration lessons to teachers.

There was an aspirational vision, a supportive culture, an instructional focus, and the active participation of the learning community. An early win — which resulted in buy-in — was the new school schedule, which was a plus for teachers because it afforded them the planning time they needed. Instructional support was provided by the professional development. And, support for the effort was ongoing through the continual involvement of coaches and continuing professional development. It is important that the effort was measured by data, which demonstrated after one semester that students were getting more credits in ELA than they had in previous years. The challenge ahead is to keep the momentum going and make sure that the training and support continue.

Now, consider the successful implementation of the vision in an urban elementary school that "all teachers are teachers of reading." The principal built on the shared values of data and trust — and everyone's high expectations for students. However, there was a cultural problem in that teachers valued autonomy and didn't share much with colleagues nor value teamwork. So there were values to build on and a big, shared value that needed to be developed.

The other big problem was that, although newer faculty members were eager to be involved, veteran teachers were more resistant. And, in all cases, faculty members couldn't visualize what all this meant in the day-to-day reality of the school. However, there was a feeling that, if this vision could be realized, it seemed logical that the extra literacy support for students would be useful. The principal was able to produce data that showed this, so most faculty members were willing to suspend disbelief and bought into trying.

The learning community played an important role here. The ELA learning community partnered with those in other subject areas for joint meetings. They arranged visits for learning community members to other schools in the district and in other cities. They developed protocols for observation. This was the early win. Schoolwide debriefing from those visits demonstrated that this approach was working effectively elsewhere and could be done in their school.

Once the goal was clear, the principal brought in professional development experts from outside provided by the district. She also modeled the teaching that was expected and reorganized the schedule so there was common planning time. This included getting subs to cover classes when the professional development was being offered.

Instructional leadership then translated into the development of several teacher leaders as coaches, available to all teachers on an ongoing basis. The assistant principal was the coach of the coaches, so they also had support.

It is now accepted practice in the school that literacy is incorporated into all classes. ELA scores have improved. This teaching practice is now rooted in the school's culture, and the ongoing support from the coaches continues.

Finally, here's an example from an urban high school with nine hundred students and eighty-four teachers. The instructional vision was to integrate mathematics in all classrooms. The vision was designed not only to improve student performance in mathematics but also to increase their perseverance in an area in which many simply gave up. If perseverance could be strengthened in mathematics, the effect should be seen in all other subjects as well—as well as benefiting students for the rest of their lives.

Accomplishing this vision required the school to share the value of the importance of mathematics for the students and the potential of all teachers to deliver such instruction. This required a culture change as well as professional development and coaching. The keys to making this work were district support, scheduling changes that permitted learning community meetings, and hiring a mathematics coach who was available to all teachers on-site.

A learning community, composed of all assistant principals and faculty members from all departments, examined the data and made a plan.

There would be common planning time every Friday from 1:20–2:35. There would be professional development for all faculty members.

The professional development—the early win—sparked interest that got the teachers excited. The common planning time and help from the coach were the ongoing supports. When students' math scores started to go up, the entire faculty celebrated—cementing the culture change. Mathematics achievement was no longer the responsibility of a single department; it was a shared responsibility across the school (and the district) and a shared success.

I realize that the illustrative stories in this chapter, and indeed throughout the book, may sound simple. We all know that they are not. It would take another full book to document the specifics of how each principal accomplished specific goals.

What they do have in common is that savvy leaders developed a vision and persevered in developing and implementing strategies that ultimately succeeded and resulted in improvements for the district, school, and students. Some of these improvements made the organization a better place to work and thereby reduced turnover of good teachers and leaders; others resulted in improved student attendance, lessened discipline referrals, and improved student learning outcomes. The strategies are most certainly not simple, but the message is that they are doable and there is an approach that works.

An effective leader starts by developing a vision and focusing on its achievement. The leader identifies the shared values of the school or district and uses them as a starting point—both to validate and further the shared values that are present and to begin to inculcate instructional values that may be missing. This begins the process of "we're all in this together."

Instructional strategies are identified that further those values and demonstrate—via early wins—the usefulness of others related to instruction that may not be present. Readiness assessments provide more information with which to plan activities that meet everyone's needs.

Schedules enable common planning time, and coaches are available for ongoing support.

More early wins and ongoing support can be realized through the creation of learning communities by which real-time learning is applied to everyone's work, and further lessons are learned and shared. Data are analyzed to assist in planning, monitoring, and ultimately evaluating the success of the strategy in achieving the vision.

The process is not linear—enter wherever it suits you and take things where they go in the context of your school or district. I hope, however, that the book has provided you with approaches, tools, pitfalls to avoid, and a sense of what others have done that inspire your success as well. Education leaders are just too important to accomplish anything less.

Annotated Bibliography

Except where noted, all publications are available for free download at www.wallacefoundation.org.

Assessing Learning-Centered Leadership: Connections to Research, Professional Standards, and Current Practices, Ellen Goldring, Andrew C. Porter, Joseph Murphy, et al., The Wallace Foundation, 2007.

Effective school leadership is key to student academic success, but the development of effective school leadership has been seriously hampered by the lack of technically sound tools to assess and monitor leader performance. A team from Vanderbilt developed such an assessment system. This paper presents the research base and conceptual framework for their learning-centered tool. The Vanderbilt assessment system contrasts with existing tools by focusing 100 percent on topics related to instructional leadership and by clearly defining and measuring the leader behaviors that can improve learning. Unlike existing tools, it also assesses individual leaders and leadership teams.

Central Office Transformation for District-Wide Teaching and Learning Improvement, Meredith I. Honig, Michael A. Copland, et al., The Wallace Foundation, 2010.

One of the first and most comprehensive studies of its kind, this report identifies five major changes that can help transform the focus of school district central offices from administration and compliance to improving classroom instruction. The report is based on an in-depth study of central office reform efforts in Atlanta, New York City, and

Oakland, California. The changes identified include the offices' strong engagement with school principals on improving instruction in their schools and the reorganizing and reculturing of every central office so it centers its work on the classroom. The report is part of a series by University of Washington researchers that investigates how leaders can contribute to improved student achievement, particularly in challenging schools and districts.

Central Office Transformation Toolkit, Meredith I. Honig, The University of Washington Center for Education Leadership, 2013.

Principals are key to improving teaching and learning in schools, but how can school district central offices give principals the support they need? Three tools designed by education researchers at the University of Washington are meant to help. Two focus on the redesign of central offices in ways that foster effective leadership in schools. The third is an aid for principal supervisors seeking to develop the instructional capabilities of the principals they oversee.

Districts Matter: Cultivating the Principals Urban Schools Need, Lee Mitgang, The Wallace Foundation, 2013.

An effective school requires an effective leader, but great principals rarely just happen; they are cultivated. This Wallace Perspective draws on a decade of foundation research and work in school leadership to show how urban school districts can play a major role in ensuring they have principals who can boost teaching and learning in troubled schools. Key actions include establishing selective hiring procedures and providing mentoring to novice leaders.

Educational Leadership Policy Standards ISLLC, The Wallace Foundation, 2008.

The development of the ISLLC (Interstate School Leader Licensure Consortium) in 1996 was a milestone in helping states and school districts define how leaders can positively influence learning and establishing guidelines to ensure that they do so. More than forty states have since adopted the ISLLC standards or used them as the basis for their own standards. In many of these states, the standards are playing an important role in informing key policies affecting the training, licensing, induction, professional development, and evaluation of school leaders. These guidelines have been revised by the Council of Chief State School Officers, applying the growth in knowledge about effective leadership practices in 2008 and will be refreshed in Fall 2015. This publication spells out the changes and their significance for improving leadership policy and practice.

Evaluation of the School Administration Manager Project, Brenda J. Turnbull, M. Bruce Haslam, et al., The Wallace Foundation, 2009.

From its beginnings in a handful of schools in Louisville, Kentucky, the School Administration Manager Project has sought to help principals delegate some of their administrative and managerial tasks and spend more of their time interacting with teachers, students, and others on instructional matters. Often, this has meant hiring a new school-level employee—a school administration manager, or SAM—to assume noninstructional tasks. This report examines the results to date of the SAM project, which involved schools in thirty-seven districts in nine states at the time of the study. The analysis, by Policy Studies Associates, finds that this approach can indeed increase the amount of time principals devote to instruction each week. But it also emphasizes the critical importance of ensuring that the project is well aligned with district improvement goals.

Getting Principal Mentoring Right: Lessons from the Field, Wallace Foundation, 2007.

Mentoring for principals during their first years on the job, once a relative rarity, is now required by half the nation's states—a major advance from a long-standing sink-or-swim attitude toward new school leaders and a belated sign of recognition of the role that well-prepared principals can play in lifting student achievement. But an analysis of this new trend by Wallace concludes that, too often, many such programs are not yet tailored to develop principals capable of driving better teaching and learning in their schools—and shaking up the status quo when necessary. Getting Principal Mentoring Right: Lessons from the

Field features close-up looks at mentoring programs in two school districts — Jefferson County Public Schools and New York City through its NYC Leadership Academy — that have put particular emphasis on getting mentoring right, with varying degrees of success to date. Based on its analysis, the report proposes several quality guidelines that might be broadly useful to states and districts thinking either about adopting new programs or improving existing ones.

How Leaders Invest Staffing Resources for Learning Improvement, Margaret L. Plecki, Michael S. Knapp, et al., The Wallace Foundation, 2009.

Urban districts and their leaders face a set of common challenges with respect to staffing high-needs schools: how to maximize the quality and longevity of high-quality teaching staff; how to deploy and support novice teachers; how to manage and minimize teacher mobility and attribution; and how to align the diversity of the teaching staff with the diversity of the student body. This report is part of a series by researchers from the University of Washington's Center for the Study of Teaching and Policy that investigates a range of topics concerned with how leaders can effectively and equitably contribute to improved student achievement, particularly in challenging school and district contexts. Based on their analyses of four urban districts and fourteen schools, the authors of this report describe a new way for school leaders to frame their decision making about staff resource allocations: "Rather than relying on the traditional pattern of isolating a funding need and allocating resources to meet that specific need, leaders need to consider the types of approaches and strategies for investing resources in coherent, effective, equitable, and sustainable ways."

How Leadership Influences Student Learning, Kenneth Leithwood, Karen Seashore Louis, Stephen Anderson, and Kyla Wahlstrom, The Wallace Foundation, 2004.

Leadership not only matters but also is second only to teaching among school-related factors that affect student learning. And its impact is greatest in schools with the greatest needs, according to a comprehensive review of evidence on school leadership by researchers at the Universities of Minnesota and Toronto. This report, the first in a series that seeks to establish how leadership promotes student achievement, summarizes the basics of successful leadership and sets out what leaders must do—including setting a clear vision, supporting and developing a talented staff, and building a solid organizational structure—to meet the challenge of school reform.

Leading Change Step-by-Step: Tactics, Tools, and Tales, Jody Spiro, Jossey–Bass, 2010.

The subject of leading change is of paramount importance for leaders these days because it seems that, more than ever, the only constant is change. It is crucial not only to have a vision but also to be skilled at translating that vision into reality and sustaining it. Leaders must know where to start, how to win support and cope with resistance, and how to institutionalize the change initiative.

Leading Change Step-by-Step offers a comprehensive and tactical guide for change leaders. It is based on field-tested approaches that have been used for more than a decade in a wide variety of organizations, including K–12 schools and districts, universities, international agencies, and nonprofits. The book is filled with proven tactics for implementing change successfully, with helpful tools to put change efforts into practice—including rubrics, helpful questions to ask, and common mistakes to avoid. Also included are stories of struggle and success that show how this approach has been used effectively in twenty-two states and internationally. The tools guide leaders through analyzing situations, identifying stakeholders, and working with them effectively to bring about the desired results.

Learning from Leadership: Investigating the Links to Improved Student Learning, Karen Seashore Louis, Kenneth Leithwood, Kyla L. Wahlstrom, et al., The Wallace Foundation, 2010.

The largest in-depth study of school leadership to date, this report gathers and analyzes quantitative data confirming that education leadership has a strong impact on student achievement as measured by student test scores. The study shows that leadership makes its mark largely by strengthening a school's professional community—an environment where teachers work together to improve classroom instruction. It also finds that rapid turnover of principals reduces student achievement. In addition, the study shows that although the principal remains the central source of leadership in schools, he or she is far from the only source. Indeed, the highest performing schools operate by a collective leadership that involves many interested players—including parents and teachers—in decision making.

Leadership for Learning Improvement in Urban Schools, Bradley S. Portin, Michael S. Knapp, et al., The Wallace Foundation, 2009.

This report is another part of a series by researchers from the University of Washington's Center for the Study of Teaching and Policy that investigates a range of topics concerned with how leaders can effectively and equitably contribute to improved student achievement, particularly in challenging school and district contexts. The questions examined in this report included (1) what it means for leaders to work in a demanding environment; (2) what supervisory leaders (principals, assistant principals, department heads) do in these kinds of settings; and (3) what nonsupervisory leaders do. Examining fifteen schools in four diverse districts, the authors conclude, among other things, that in these demanding settings, principals need to behave as "leaders of instructional teams, as much as individual instructional leaders."

Make Room for the Principal Supervisors, Jennifer Gill, The Wallace Foundation, 2013.

This story from the field describes how Denver Public Schools hired more people to coach and evaluate its principals—despite tight budgets. A major feature of the district's overhaul was what's known in the business world as "reducing the span of control," or decreasing the number of people a supervisor manages so he or she can better support each one.

Making Time for Instructional Leadership, Ellen Goldring, Ellen Goldring, Jason A. Grissom, Christine M. Neumerski, Joseph Murphy, Richard Blissett and Andy Porter, The Wallace Foundation, July 2015.

This report describes the "SAM process," an approach that about 700 schools around the nation are using to direct more of principals' time and effort to improve teaching and learning in classrooms. Research has shown that a principal's instructional leadership is second only to teaching among school-related influences on student success. But principals often find themselves mired in matters of day-to-day administration and have little time to cultivate better teachers who can help students learn. The SAM process is designed to free up principals' time so they can focus on improving instruction in classrooms.

Rethinking Leadership: The Changing Role of Principal Supervisors, Amanda Corcoran, Michael Casserly, et al., The Wallace Foundation, 2013.

This report, among the first to provide a detailed look at the principal supervisor role, finds that these administrators often face daunting problems in carrying out their jobs effectively—including having to oversee too many schools (an average of twenty-four). The report offers recommendations for how districts can improve matters. One suggestion is to make sure supervisors are matched with schools suitable to their skills and expertise.

School Leadership in Action: Principal Practices, WNET, The Wallace Foundation, 2015.

This video series follows 10 principals in four metropolitan areas through their workdays, showing how they use the five practices of effective school leadership to improve teaching and learning in their classrooms.

Shaping a Vision of Academic Success for all Students: A Roadmap of key Processes and Effective Practice. Lawrenceville: Georgia: Georgia Leadership Institute for School Improvement, The Wallace Foundation, January 2015.

This handbook, written by eight principals from urban districts, offers advice from those in the field about the important role played by setting an inspirational vision for the school community. The authors also provide experience-based advice on how to develop a vision and put into action.

The School Principal as Leader: Guiding Schools to Better Teaching and Learning, The Wallace Foundation, 2013.

This Wallace Foundation publication summarizes a decade of research and work in school leadership to identify what it is that effective school principals do. It concludes that they carry out five key actions particularly well, including shaping a vision of academic success for all students and cultivating leadership in others.

Ideas for Using These Materials in Courses and Workshops

Many readers of this book provide professional development for education leaders. Here are some ideas, by topic, for that purpose. Below are suggestions that could comprise a full semester graduate course or portions thereof. Of course, any topics may be used for individual workshops.

One way to use the materials is to have the topic discussion in one session and ask participants to use the tool or exercise in-between sessions, bring back the result and discuss their experience. What follows are some discussion questions by topic:

Topic 1: The Role of Education Leaders (Chapter 1)

1. Who is the most effective education leader you have worked with? Why?

2. What leadership teams exist in your schools and/or districts? Who are their members? What do they do? What results have they achieved?

3. Is "sharing leadership" a realistic goal? Have you seen this in action? What does it look like when done well?

4. Do you agree that leadership is "second only" to teaching among school-related factors for student learning? Why or why not?

Topic 2: Change Leadership (Chapter 1)

1. It has been argued that assessing "readiness" for change is an important first step, yet it is often skipped. Why do you think this happens?

2. If readiness is low, should you abandon the proposed change or can you realistically improve readiness?

3. Do you agree that people generally hear the need for change as "blaming"? Can you think of an example where you have experienced or observed this?

4. Why is it important to consider the potential sustainability of any reform from the beginning? Have you seen this happen? What was the effect of doing so?

Topic 3: Vision and Focus (Chapter 2)

1. What makes a good vision statement? What does it look like when a vision is really translated into daily operations?

2. How can an effective leader facilitate others to focus on priorities? Is it realistic to remove lesser priorities from other people's plates?

3. What percent of time would you estimate that you (or your principal) spend on matters directly related to improving instruction? How do you know?

4. What data might tell you whether you, as leader, are sufficiently focused on your change goal?

Topic 4: Culture (Chapters 3 and 4)

1. Is it a contradiction to say that culture both "evolves" and is led? Give an example of both aspects you have observed.

2. Give an example you have experienced or observed of how upsetting the culture derailed something important in your school or district. Could this have been prevented? How?

3. Do you agree that people's personal values play a role in the culture – even if those values have little to do with instruction-centered beliefs?

4. What are the various organizational cultures at play in your school or district? Have you observed or experienced a discrepancy between or among them (perhaps creating conflicts for individuals who are members of different organizational cultures simultaneously)? How did this play out? How can a leader reconcile differences?

Topic 5: Improving Instruction (Chapters 5 and 6)

1. What has been the most effective instructional improvement strategy in which you have participated? What made it so effective? How did you know?

2. What strategies are most effective in supporting adults to improve their practice? How can a leader provide these supports?

3. What is the role of effective teacher evaluation in improving instruction? What is the role of or on-going coaching?

4. What supports can the district office provide for school leaders in improving instruction? How can the district office remove barriers?

Topic 6: Learning Communities (Chapters 7 and 8)

1. What learning communities are active in your school or district? Who participates? What do they do?

2. How is time found for learning communities to meet? What structures exist?

3. What is the best example of a learning community in which you have participated and/or led? Why did it work so well?

4. Give an example of something currently operational in the school or district that was developed by a learning community.

Topic 7: Using all Strategies Together (Chapter 9)

1. In the examples from Chapter 9, how did all three high-payoff strategies work together? Give examples of each strategy and how it worked in concert with the others to achieve the result.

2. Analyze a successful change in which you have participated. Were any of the high-payoff strategies in evidence? If so, what were they and how did they work together?

3. Looking forward, think of a change you would like to see happen in your school or district. Which of the high-payoff strategies would you use, and how could they be sequenced?

4. If you could only use one high-payoff strategy, which would it be and why?

Name Index

Anderson, S., 130

Blissett, R., 133

Casserly, M., 133
Copland, M. A., 127
Corcoran, A., 133

Gill, J., 132
Goldring, E., 127, 133
Grissom, J. A., 133

Haslam, M. B., 129
Honig, M. I., 127, 128

Knapp, M. S., 130, 132

Leithwood, K., 130, 131
Louis, K. S., 3, 6–8, 93, 129–131

Maslow, A., 99
Mitgang, L., 128
Murphy, J., 127, 133

Neumerski, C. M., 133

Plecki, M. L., 130
Porter, A. C., 6, 127, 133
Portin, B. S., 132

Spiro, J., 131

Turnbull, B. J., 129

Wahlstrom, K., 130, 131

Index

A

Assessing Attitudes and Aptitudes (AAA) tool: defined, 76; and instructional improvement strategy, 77; items in, 79–84; useful analyses of, 78, 85–87

Assessment of student progress, 76, 84

Assistant principals, 23

Assumptions: leader's, 41–42; testing, 47, 51

B

Bulletin boards, 31

Buy-in: importance of, 8; and instructional leadership, 67–68; and learning communities, 98–99; and personal experience, 47; and school culture, 35–36

C

Change leadership, effective, 9–11

Classroom walkthroughs, 63

Climate, defined, 5

Coaches, instructional: importance of, 70; ongoing support from, 124

Coaching: facilitating as, 100; observing without, 71

Crisis management, 23

Culture, school: buy-in for, 35–36; defined, 32; invisible, 39–40; leading, 38–39; principal-driven, 36; and shared values, 33–34; supportive of teaching and learning 5–6; and symbols, 32–33; tool for measuring, 48–57

Culture Responsiveness Task Force, 39

Curriculum development, 76, 81–82

D

Data: at district level, 75–76; graduation, 75; importance of, 75; tool for collecting and analyzing, 76–87

Data team, 107

Discussions, leaders dominating, 102–103

District vision statement, 17, 18

District-level learning communities, 96–97

E

Early win: as building block, 8–9; for instructional improvement, 69–70; new school schedule as, 123; professional development as, 125; for supportive culture, 36–37

Education concepts and philosophies, 76, 80

Educator attitudes, assessing: AAA tool for, 76; and instructional improvement strategy, 77; survey items for, 79–84; and useful analyses of data, 78, 85–87

R

Reflective journals, 64
Resources, aligning, 20, 26

S

SAM (school administration manager) process, 21, 22
School culture: buy-in for, 35–36; defined, 32; invisible, 39–40; leading, 38–39; principal-driven, 36; and shared values, 33–34; supportive of teaching and learning 5–6; and symbols, 32–33
School leadership: important aspects of, 4; and improved student achievement, 3; three high-payoff strategies for, 5, 121–126
School vision statement, 17, 18
Self-reflective tool for leaders, 24, 25–26
Signs and bulletin boards, 31
Strategies, high-payoff: building blocks for, 8–9; combining, 121–126; defined, 4, 5; instructional improvements, 5, 6–7, 63–72; learning communities, 5, 7–8, 93–103; supportive culture, 5–6, 29–43
Student achievement, and school leadership, 3
Student learning, principles of, 76, 81
Student progress, assessment of, 76, 84
Support, ongoing: importance of, 9; and instructional leadership, 70, 124; and shared values, 37–38
Symbols: importance of, 42–43; shared values as, 34–35; use of, 32–33

T

Teacher resistance, and instructional improvement, 67–68, 123
Teachers, avoiding underperforming, 72
Templates, learning together: facilitator's template, 113–114; general description of, 107–108; learning community planner's template, 111–113; participants' needs assessment template, 109–110; and sample work plan, 115
Three high-payoff strategies: building blocks for, 8–9; combining, 121–126; defined, 4, 5; instructional improvements, 5, 6–7, 63–72; learning communities, 5, 7–8, 93–103; supportive culture, 5–6, 29–43
Time management, 20, 21–23

U

Underperforming teachers, avoiding, 72

V

Values: awareness of, 40–41, 47, 48, 51; discussing, 54; instruction-centered, 33, 57; in measuring-the-culture tool, 49–57; number one, 56; rating, 51–52; restoring, 53; summary template, 55
Values, shared: and actions, 33–34; and ongoing support, 37–38; as symbols, 34–35
Vision: and focus, 19–26; importance of, 5; self-reflection on, 25–26; setting the, 16–18; three high-payoff strategies for achieving, 121–126; two examples of, 18–19